TALENT ASSESSMENT AND TECHNIQUES

The key to understanding and optimising assessments in the workplace

Dr Belinda Board & Daniel de Freitas

TALENT MANAGEMENT SERIES

Table of Contents

About the Authors

Dr Belinda Board is the CEO of PeopleWise and an Associate Fellow of the British Psychological Society (BPS). She is a Chartered Clinical Psychologist with postgraduate degrees in organisational and forensic psychology and a PhD in leadership behaviours and workplace well-being. As a leading psychologist and executive coach to the business world, Belinda blends her deep psychological expertise with 20 years' experience of working with business leaders around the globe, to enable deep and sustainable growth of psychological capabilities that are critical for individuals and organisations to thrive and succeed. Belinda has built up extensive experience in the design and delivery of global end-to-end talent management solutions. She is a global specialist in organisational transformation, behaviourally anchored assessment, executive coaching, strategic thinking, cultural diversity, psychometric tool design and leadership development. Belinda's research into leadership behaviours and workplace well-being has been published in a variety of peer-reviewed journals. She is currently engaged with the University of Surrey and Florida Atlantic University on joint research projects that are investigating workplace well-being and leadership potential respectively.

Daniel de Freitas (CPsychol) is the Head of Talent Assessment and Principal Business Psychologist at PeopleWise, registered as a Chartered Psychologist with the British Psychological Society (BPS) in the United Kingdom and Organisational Psychologist registered with the Health Professions Council in South Africa (HPCSA). Daniel has designed and delivered end-to-end strategic and operational talent management initiatives across the globe. With a background in organisational psychology, consulting, talent management and human resource management, Daniel has over 13 years of business experience across different industries including the Retail, Financial Services, Banking, Mining, Petroleum, Telecommunication and Health Care sectors including Human Resources & Business Consulting. Daniel has successfully worked as an internal talent manager, as well as an external talent partner, by partnering with individuals at all levels, allowing him to understand the full impact of business decisions, not only at a leadership level, but also on those who are required to execute on the strategy, both of which ultimately impact on performance. After completing his Masters degree in Organisational Psychology (with Distinction), he went on to pursue a Coaching Diploma, and a course in Business Competency through the London School of Business and Finance, in order to integrate psychology, coaching and business practices. He is currently completing his PhD in Psychology.

Introduction

In the increasingly volatile, uncertain, complex and ambiguous (VUCA) world which organisations are operating in, it is absolutely business-critical to ensure that your organisation's assessment strategies and processes are in line with best practice and effectively contribute to talent, human resource (HR) and business strategy.

After years of research, implementation and refinement, psychometric and non-psychometric assessments are acknowledged to assist in identifying, retaining and developing talent more objectively.

Sound assessment practices ultimately contribute to identifying strengths and development areas of individuals and thereby help sift which candidates are best matched to join and grow your organisation.

Who is this book for?

This is an essential read for every CEO, HR Executive and Talent Manager who seeks to further their understanding of the role assessments have as business drivers. It also offers best practice guidelines to refresh knowledge on assessments and optimise their assessment practices that contribute to talent and human resource strategy in the workplace.

Using this book

Not to be used in isolation. It is critical that assessments form part of the selection and development processes, and should not be the only data point for deciding to hire or develop employees.

Flowchart for Talent Assessment and Techniques

Chapter 1: Understanding the past to predict the future	**Chapter 2:** The business case for utilising assessments	**Chapter 3:** Assessments across the globe
Chapter 4: An overview of the different types of assessments	**Chapter 5:** Psychometric assessments	**Chapter 6:** Non-psychometric assessments
Chapter 7: An overview of assessment and development centres	**Chapter 8:** The predictive power of assessments	**Chapter 9:** Optimising the candidate experience

Chapter 1

Understanding the past to predict the future

THIS CHAPTER COVERS:

- The evolution of assessments in the war for talent
- The latest trends in talent
- Designing the workforce of the future

The evolution of assessments in the war for talent

Many organisations overlook the fact that their staff, particularly their top quartile talent, is arguably their most valuable and important asset. However, the realisation of talent being an asset is not enough. Over several years, research has demonstrated the link between placing the right candidate, in the right role, at the right time and the degree of value this brings to organisations.

If we consider talent to be an asset then we also need to consider not only the benefits that this brings but also the risks associated with identifying, retaining and maintaining talent.

Despite the established link between investment in talent management and increased performance, we know that many organisations continue to implement human resource policies and people strategies which lack talent management as a key priority or strategic driver.

As a result, many organisations are struggling to answer questions such as:

1. How do we attract the right talent?
2. Which candidate will best fit our culture?
3. How do we know who will be a successful candidate when they all seem so good on paper?
4. Why should we invest in assessments if CVs and references give us a good idea of the candidate's ability to do the job?
5. How could we have identified earlier, that this individual was not the right fit?
6. What does "potential" mean in our organisation and how do we accurately measure it?
7. What does great leadership look like?
8. Why are talented people leaving?

We have all been on the receiving end of such questions and have worked in organisations where management has relied solely on CVs and interviews as their main selection tools. Although some research supports the notion that certain job-related competencies can be identified through CV screening, this requires trained individuals who know what to look for and an objective lens to inform decisions throughout the recruitment process.

A little history

In the 1950s, internal talent development existed with many of the methods we utilise today-albeit in a different way-and was focused mainly at the middle management level. In the 1970s, internal talent development began to fall away when companies were starting to realise that it was not keeping up with the rate of change experienced in the business world, as middle managers were being trained and groomed to occupy more senior positions in the near future with less roles available.

This was further evidenced during the economic downturn of the 1980s, as succession pipelines were no longer accurately aligned with the business needs of that time. Additionally, there was an oversupply of middle managers, who were on succession plans and were undergoing development, with less jobs available for developed employees to fill. Some larger organisations retained the practice of talent development and were known as "academy companies" just for maintaining the practices that had been in place, which most other companies had discarded.

In the early 1990s, as business started to increase, companies were relying heavily on hiring talent from outside the organisation as they had a wide range of talent to choose from due to the large pool of developed middle managers who were laid off as a result of the recession. Mid-1990s organisations were noticing that talented employees were being headhunted by competitors, as the external talent pool began to run dry due to talented employees being actively recruited as economies across the globe continued to grow.[1]

What's in the name "talent"?

The word "talent" dates to ancient Greece starting as a measure of weight, then becoming a unit of money, and later meaning a person's value or natural abilities.[2]

In 1998, the *McKinsey Quarterly* published the well-known paper, "The War for Talent", which looked at 77 large companies in the United States (US) and concluded that "Companies are about to be engaged in a war for senior executive talent that will remain a defining characteristic of their competitive landscape for decades to come. Yet most are ill prepared, and even the best are vulnerable".[3]

This paper spotlighted the need to see and treat talent and employees as human capital and not just resources. For some it was an awakening to the fact that talented employees are a valuable commodity, critical to ensuring business success. This article catapulted the need for talent management to the forefront of many companies' strategic agendas and hence talent development, assessment and succession planning re-emerged, not just for middle managers but for employees across differing levels of management, as well as employees belonging to different specialisms.

Today, talent encompasses a much wider range of individuals than previously covered in the middle management arena. Talent can be defined across several different platforms such as having scarce skills, requisite characteristics, experience, knowledge and/or leadership qualities. While the defining characteristics of talent have evolved, many companies still rely on outdated and relatively poor predictors of assessing talent such as sifting through CVs, conducting unstructured interviews and contacting references.

What is Talent Management?

"An integrated set of processes, programs and cultural norms in an organization designed and implemented to attract, develop, deploy, and retain talent to achieve strategic objectives and meet future business needs."[4]

Assessments began to surface at the start of World War I which introduced the "science of selection" as a primary selection process under the arm of human factors research. The first assessment during this time was done by a team of psychologists headed up by Robert Yerkes, president of the American Psychological Association (APA) who carried out the first recorded adult intelligence tests on army recruits. These tests were labelled Army Alpha and Army Beta tests. The Alpha test was a verbal test for literate personnel (featured as Alpha Test Excerpt) and the Beta test was developed for non-verbal administration for those who were illiterate and for non-English speakers (Beta Test Excerpt).[5]

Despite criticism of being biased, some determined the use of these assessments as a huge success, as the US military administered these 'intelligence' tests to more than 1.7 million army recruits.[6] The work done by Yerkes and his team initiated the use of psychological testing for vocational purposes and the principle of standardised testing as seen in testing practices utilised today.[7]

This is a test of common sense. Below are sixteen questions. Three answers are given to each question. You are to look at the answers carefully; then make a cross in the square before the best answer to each question, as in the sample:

SAMPLE
Why do we use stoves? Because
☐ they look well
☒ they keep us warm
☐ they are black

Here the second answer is the best one and is marked with a cross. Begin with No. 1 and keep on until time is called.

1 It is wiser to put some money aside and not spend it all, so that you may
☐ prepare for old age or sickness
☐ collect all the different kinds of money
☐ gamble when you wish

2 Shoes are made of leather, because
☐ it is tanned
☐ it is tough, pliable and warm
☐ it can be blackened

3 Why do soldiers wear wrist watches rather than pocket watches? Because
☐ they keep better time
☐ they are harder to break
☐ they are handier

4 The main reason why stone is used for building purposes is because
☐ it makes a good appearance
☐ it is strong and lasting
☐ it is heavy

5 Why is beef better food than cabbage? Because
☐ it tastes better
☐ it is more nourishing
☐ it is harder to obtain

6 If some one does you a favor, what should you do?
☐ try to forget it
☐ steal for him if he asks you to
☐ return the favor

7 If you do not get a letter from home, which you know was written, it may be because
☐ it was lost in the mails
☐ you forgot to tell your people to write
☐ the postal service has been discontinued

8 The main thing the farmers do is to
☐ supply luxuries
☐ make work for the unemployed
☐ feed the nation
☞ Go to No. 9 above

9 If a man who can't swim should fall into a river, he should
☐ yell for help and try to scramble out
☐ dive to the bottom and crawl out
☐ lie on his back and float

10 Glass insulators are used to fasten telegraph wires because
☐ the glass keeps the pole from being burned
☐ the glass keeps the current from escaping
☐ the glass is cheap and attractive

11 If your load of coal gets stuck in the mud, what should you do?
☐ leave it there
☐ get more horses or men to pull it out
☐ throw off the load

12 Why are criminals locked up?
☐ to protect society
☐ to get even with them
☐ to make them work

13 Why should a married man have his life insured? Because
☐ death may come at any time
☐ insurance companies are usually honest
☐ his family will not then suffer if he dies

14 In Leap Year February has 29 days because
☐ February is a short month
☐ some people are born on February 29th
☐ otherwise the calendar would not come out right

15 If you are held up and robbed in a strange city, you should
☐ apply to the police for help
☐ ask the first man you meet for money to get home
☐ borrow some money at a bank

16 Why should we have Congressmen? Because
☐ the people must be ruled
☐ it insures truly representative government
☐ the people are too many to meet and make their laws

Plate III. Alpha Test 3: Practical Judgment (Form 8).

Figure 1: Alpha Test Excerpt[8]

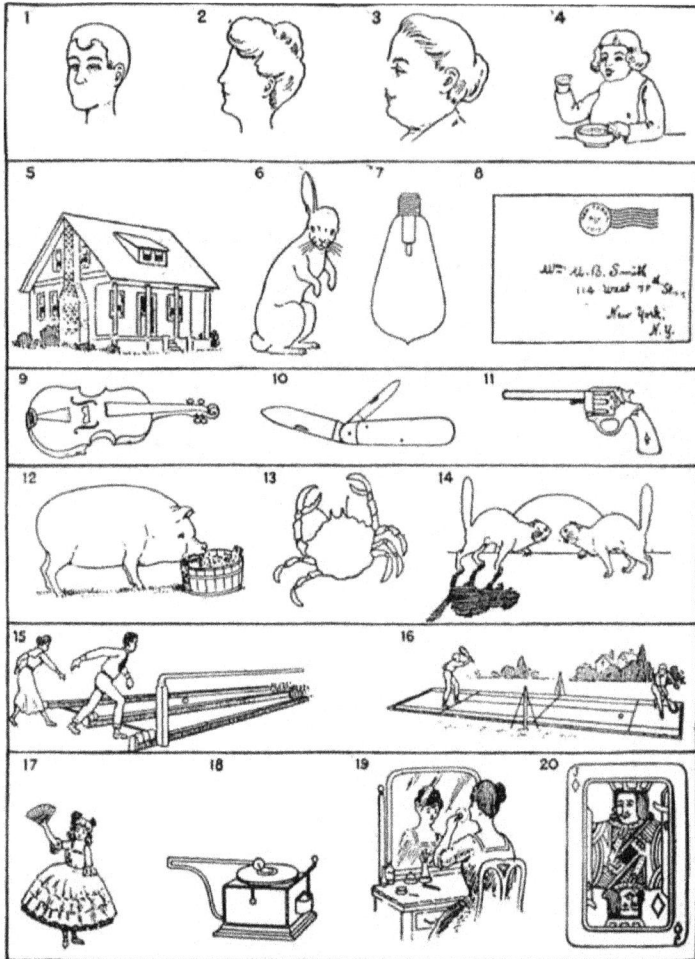

Figure 2: Beta Test Excerpt[9]

The introduction of the Alpha and Beta tests led to an increase in the number of assessment practices. Similarly, more providers entered the private market, however, many of them used unscientific techniques purporting to assess people's personality and intellect. These included assessments such as palm reading, phrenology (assessment of skull protrusions), assessment of head size, physiognomy (assessment of facial features) and/or graphology as pseudo-science methods of selection.[10]

In order to increase employees' and employers' belief in these tests and to add a level of rigour to science-based assessments, the APA carried out extensive research in psychological and educational testing which resulted in the establishment of two key assessment evaluation metrics that form the cornerstone of psychometric assessments utilised today: reliability and validity (described in more detail in chapter 4).[11]

Reliability refers to the stability of a construct to remain relatively unchanged and produce similar results when re-assessed on different occasions. Validity refers to the degree to which an instrument assesses what it claims to measure.

To establish adequate reliability and validity outcomes for assessments, large amounts of data are required. Additionally, when developing an assessment, a lot more items than are utilised need to be included in the testing. Due to the use of unregulated assessments, the increased time required to develop reliable and valid assessments, together with the high unemployment rates associated with the Great Depression, the use of scientifically validated pre-screening tests declined and only regained popularity around the time of World War II.[12]

World War II brought assessments back into the public eye with the introduction of the following assessments:

- The Wonderlic Personnel Test (WPT) – created in 1936 as the first short-form cognitive abilities test, by E.F. Wonderlic, which was utilised to assist the US Navy to select candidates for pilot training and navigation. It was further utilised in the Douglas Aircraft Corporation to solve employee placement and training problems.

- The Cardall Test of Practical Judgment – created in 1942 as the first situational judgement test, by Alfred Cardall, proposed to measure problem-solving ability in everyday life.

- *The Briggs-Myers Type Indicator Handbook* – created in 1944 as the precursor to the Myers-Briggs test, was created by mother-daughter duo Katharine Cook Briggs and Isabel Briggs Myers to evaluate personality.

The renewed focus on personality and cognitive testing, coupled with the covert operational needs of the Office of Strategic Services (OSS, the precursor to the CIA), led to the development of physical assessment centres.

During World War II, the OSS ran assessments ranging from pencil-and-paper tests to more complex tests of skill such as situational judgement tests. A notable situational test, named the Construction Situation, required candidates to supervise and instruct two uncooperative privates, as the privates built a miniature house. At the close of the war, the use of assessment centres continued with a shift in focus to industrial and vocational applications instead.[13]

The Construction Situation

Figure 3: The Construction Situation

With the increased use of assessments, for employment purposes, landmark legislation in the US defined how assessments would be utilised moving forward. The Civil Rights Act of 1964 was instituted and further landmark cases such as the ruling of Griggs vs. Duke Power (1971), illustrated the need to eliminate bias and discrimination from employment practices, specifically based on race, colour, nation origin, religion or sex.[14]

"In the case Griggs vs. Duke Power (1971), the Supreme Court established specific rules for job selection tests:

1. Selection tests must be job related and based on the qualifications of the specific job;
2. If adverse impact occurs, the employer must demonstrate that the test is job related."[15]

Many of the paper assessments developed during the late 1980s are still available today with the major shifts being in the delivery of these assessments from paper-and-pencil to telephonic and online forms.

In 1996, the first online assessment for selection was launched, which has since seen the likes of many different assessments being developed and major assessment providers offering online solutions in addition to paper-and-pencil versions.

> According to Talent Board's 2016 Candidate Experience Research Report, over 82% of companies are utilising some form of pre-screening assessment tool.[16]

The use of assessments has progressed through the ages, with some geographies implementing stricter guidelines which govern their use for selection purposes. Despite stricter regulations, a large majority of companies are utilising assessments as part of the selection process. With 80% of talent open to new opportunities and companies spending $4000/R61 410/£3315 on average per candidate through scheduling, interviewing and assessments, the war for talent and the need for objective, predictive assessments is higher than ever.[17]

The latest trends in talent management

Some of the top trends in talent management in 2019 include:

1. Realigning and redesigning jobs to meet the requirements of future roles

With the implementation of new technologies to drive assessment and selection processes forward, it is no surprise that advances have been made to assist in redesigning job descriptions and the skills required for those roles. Most people are familiar with the study that has been published, defining the skills required for the 2020 workforce, yet in 2019 many job adverts do not include these skills as requirements or prerequisites and job adverts have not changed much over the last decade.

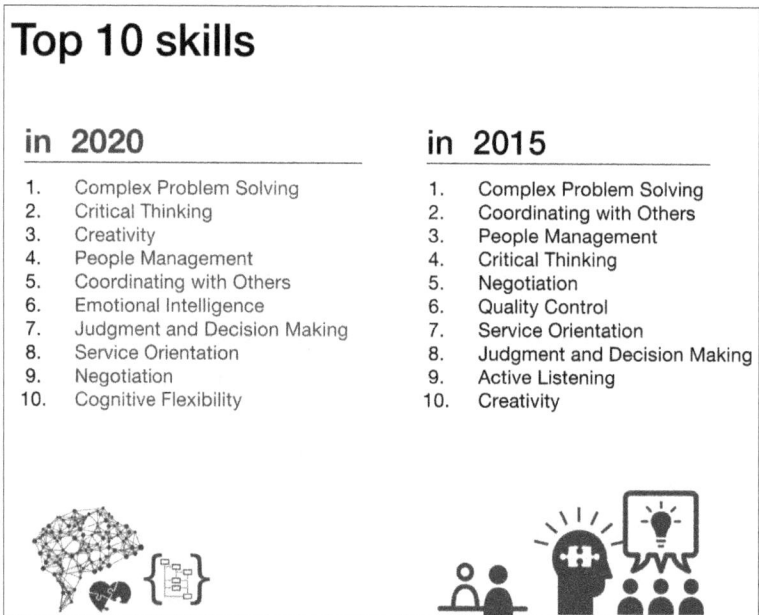

Top 10 skills

in 2020	in 2015
1. Complex Problem Solving	1. Complex Problem Solving
2. Critical Thinking	2. Coordinating with Others
3. Creativity	3. People Management
4. People Management	4. Critical Thinking
5. Coordinating with Others	5. Negotiation
6. Emotional Intelligence	6. Quality Control
7. Judgment and Decision Making	7. Service Orientation
8. Service Orientation	8. Judgment and Decision Making
9. Negotiation	9. Active Listening
10. Cognitive Flexibility	10. Creativity

Figure 4: World Economic Forum's Top 10 Skills[18]

With the help of internal talent managers, with some companies seeking the skills of external talent partners, some organisations are redefining human capital trends by reviewing their current and required roles for the future – some of which include the critical skills outlined in the 2020 report. Some companies are fearful, while others are sceptical, of the impact that artificial intelligence (AI) will have on the global workforce while others are using AI to their advantage. As with the fear of the internet, the fear of AI replacing jobs is on the mind of many employees and employers. However, much like the introduction of the internet, we mostly observed job roles being redefined to include more meaningful work for humans.

In the age of the VUCA world, job roles cannot be static definitions of how employees should operate, as the world is constantly changing. Therefore, job roles, as well as employees, need to support change, as well as pre-empt the disruptions that are imminent as part of the changing world. As job roles are being defined, it requires HR practitioners not only to establish which roles are critical but also which roles are repetitive, strategic, perennial, project-based and/ or can be replaced by AI. This has changed the 'build' and 'buy' strategies that exist in the HR world, referring to the building of talent within the organisation and the buying of talent from outside the organisation respectively, to the more contemporary phrase: 'build, buy, borrow or bot'. 'Borrow' refers to the use of freelancers or consultants to undertake work that is required and 'bot' refers to roles that can be undertaken by automation or AI.

In redefining roles, many practitioners interchangeably misuse the terms "automation"' and "AI" by referring to tasks that can be automated and/or replaced by AI.

Automation refers to tasks that are repetitive and/or can be duplicated by software, and/or hardware, as there is a sequential flow in the order of how things are done. There is very little to no human intervention required in carrying out these tasks as there is no decision making that needs to occur. An example includes a production line where cars are being produced. Many of these practices are automated as operators simply need to ensure the product lines are working and producing products based on quality assurance standards.

When we refer to tasks or roles that can be replaced by AI, we are referring to the use of software or hardware which is governed by algorithms which assist in carrying out the tasks. These algorithms are coding equations built by software developers that have decision trees built into them, much like 'if-then' statements. For example, we have seen the introduction of AI in social media screening which proposes to remove bias from the process. This software is said to screen a candidate's social media posts, and social media presence, to produce scores on several different factors, which are linked to the workplace.

While the algorithms which govern these kinds of software are usually kept secret to prevent replication, we can imagine that a task could be created using software and coding to search for negative and positive words to determine if a person is more negative or positive in their approach to life. There are obvious concerns and critiques of the use of AI for these kinds of endeavours, such as the use of personal data to inform selection decisions, especially without consent, but on the other side of the coin, most users of the internet and apps do not read the terms and conditions of the content which they post – as was evident with the concerns of an app that the public was using to transform their faces to see what they would look like in their old age. Little did they know that by uploading their faces they were giving the owners of the app the rights to utilise their faces for future advertising without limitation.

2. Capitalising on talent analytics

Organisations have one of the most valuable sources of information available at their fingertips which many researchers would pay to access – data of individuals over a prolonged period of time. This is longitudinal data on employees which spans over a period and has many data points relating to individuals who are currently and were part of the organisation at some point. This data can include

HR metrics such as absenteeism, performance data and training attendance, as well as assessment data and employee engagement data. The rise of talent analytics has resulted in data being as important as business analytics: How do you get business results without the right people?

Talent analytics refers to the compilation and analysis of this data to inform talent management strategy within the organisation. Some of the most valuable uses of this data have been to inform:[19]

1.   The effectiveness of training interventions;
2.   When to build, buy or borrow talent;
3.   Key drivers of engagement;
4.   The candidates who are likely to serve longer tenures;
5.   Employees at risk of burnout.

Smaller companies will tend to have fewer data points to work with. As was mentioned when discussing the history of assessments, the more data points available, the more useful the results are. Therefore, larger organisations that have been around for many years and have successfully tracked their data will be able to provide more insights into their previous and current workforce. Imagine the possibilities of having objective data from across organisations relating to when an individual started work, HR data and performance data which could then assist in producing outcome variables that may help shape the way organisations do business and manage talent today.

3.   Understanding what EVP factors contribute to tenure

A study which was conducted by Mercer[20] in 2018 illustrated the value that each generation (Generation Y, Generation X and Baby Boomers) placed on various aspects of what contributed to them remaining at their workplace. Generation Y includes individuals born between 1980 and 1994 (also known as millennials), Generation X refers to those born between 1965 and 1979 and the Baby Boomer generation includes individuals born between 1946 and 1964.

While all three generations show high value for job security, Generation Y showed higher value for a fun work environment, advanced opportunities and professional development compared to the other two generations. Generation X showed higher values for time off and flexible working hours while Baby Boomers showed higher value for meaningful work, competitive pay, convenient location, and health benefits.[21]

When looking at the results it is interesting to see the differences between the different generations, but it is also important to keep in mind that there will also be differences based on other factors such as management level, gender and socio-economic status to name a few.

4. Global top three drivers to help employees thrive

The key drivers per country were tabled in understanding what the three most important factors were, to help employees thrive in the workplace according to the global talent trend study published by Mercer.[22] The study shows that the top three drivers will differ based on where you are in the world but globally the following three factors are said to drive employee performance:[23]

1. The ability to manage work-life balance
2. Recognition for contributions made
3. Ability to learn new skills and technologies

Organisations that wish to be global players in the talent space should consider adjustments relating to the above, even if the study mentioned above is used as a platform to have open discussions about what truly matters to your employees.

5. Top HR AI initiatives

With the use of AI, organisations are not only adapting and redesigning roles in the workplace, but HR departments are using AI to assist with tasks that may be unnecessarily complex and labour-intensive. Some of the functions that are being spearheaded by AI technology include:[24]

1. Improving employee self-service using chatbots
2. Identifying employees at risk of leaving
3. Recommending job openings and career paths
4. Forming part of the performance management process
5. Customising employee compensation and improving benchmarking

Some of the investments in AI to enable HR departments to make better decisions is likely to increase, as AI proves to provide this information at a faster and potentially cheaper rate in the long run, when compared to hiring external consultants.

6. Diversity and inclusion

Diversity and inclusion has been 'a priority' on the list of many organisations but in the western world, where diversity appears to still be focused on gender equality, we must keep in mind that this is not the only form of diversity. There is a plethora of richness and difference of opinion that can be gained and leveraged by promoting a workforce that accounts for diversity amongst general workers and leadership by also acknowledging the value of difference that comes with nationality, race, sexual orientation, religion, socio-economic status, disability, location, and age to name a few. When organisations truly embrace these differences and promote inclusions and idea-sharing through learning cultures, increased levels of innovation will start to emerge as you build out a global organisation.[25]

Designing the workforce of the future

We live in a world characterised by information overload, rapid pace, continual change, and global reach; therefore, today's businesses must think and behave differently. The successful organisation must be designed to be fast-paced, agile and resilient in order to compete and win in today's global business; environment.

The technological advances and economic development are pushing companies to re-think strategies and re-shape the way they design jobs, organise work, and plan for future growth. Nowadays the focus has shifted towards dividing the human and non-human aspects of work. Whilst certain tasks are being carried out by AI, capabilities like empathy, communication, persuasion, personal service, problem-solving, and strategic decision making may still require human intervention. While people and tasks can be separated, the rules according to which we design our future world of work have changed. These changes may impact the way we see our organisation and may require us to shift our mindset to accommodate the changes and utilise them to our benefit.

The development of the future workforce depends on reshaping your company, which means future-proofing your organisation. Despite the increased adoption of AI, only 17% of executives believe they are ready to manage an organisation comprised of people, AI, and robots[17]. Additionally, only 11% of companies believe that they understand how to build the organisation of the future.[26] One place to start would be to review and redesign critical roles and those most likely to be impacted by AI and build out how they link to the wider organisation through a common, overarching competency framework.

Table 1: The future world of work: Old rules vs. new rules[27]

Old rules	New rules
Machines and artificial intelligence are replacing jobs.	Jobs and tasks are being redesigned and split into human and non-human tasks.
Main talent source is full-time employees.	Talent is available from multiple sources such as contractors, temporary workers, gig employees, part-time and full-time employees.
Workforce planning focuses on the skills of full-time employees.	Workforce planning considers the tasks required and analyses the various skills and options across multiple workforces and technologies.
Jobs are static with fixed skill requirements.	The relevance of some skills continues to decrease as work is constantly being reinvented.
Jobs and career paths are the foundation of work and the workforce.	Projects, tasks and assignments inform the building blocks of work and the workforce required.
Robotics and cognitive technologies are projects for the IT department.	Integrating technology and people is of relevance across the organisation as a multidisciplinary task.
HR's job in automation is to focus on change management and workforce transition.	HR being more strategic in facilitating the redesign of jobs and training the augmented workforce.
The fundamental elements of work are jobs described in job descriptions.	The fundamental elements of work are tasks aggregated into jobs and roles.

When identifying critical roles that are necessary for the functioning and success of the business, start to plot out whether these roles fall under the categories build, buy, borrow or bot. As you start to identify and build-out the list of critical roles, you can then look at the job profiles of those roles to determine if they are still fit for purpose or whether they need to be redesigned or edited to encompass the role as it currently stands but also for the future.

If you prefer to take a different approach, think about the roles and tasks that add less or little value to the organisation but take up a great deal of time to complete – these may be the ideal tasks to get automated, introduce AI or even look at borrowing the talent to come in only when needed. This analysis also allows you to work from a systemic approach by looking at which tasks touch which roles, also allowing you to think of new roles that can be created through consolidation and allowing individuals to take on roles that involve more meaningful work.

Once you have an idea of the most important or most impacted roles, how are you going to redesign them? Best practice would be to utilise a competency framework to which all roles should link back.

Most companies today have a competency framework in place which defines the prerequisite behaviours, aptitudes, technical expertise, values and/or skills that individuals need to perform their roles. Competency frameworks should be living models that adapt and change as the organisation and its employees are required to. The framework provides the foundation to which employers and employees can refer in shaping individual development plans relating to each of the roles.

In the current VUCA world, it would be ideal for a framework to encompass aspects of change, unpredictability and adaptation so as to allow for the organisation not only to embrace change but to plan for it and be agile enough to adapt to whatever changes the company is faced with. Some organisations will build out their competency framework in line with their vision and values, tying it off with the recruitment and internal development processes to ensure that the framework is applied from hire to retire. Other companies will utilise existing universal frameworks which consist of hundreds of competencies and options to choose from in putting together the framework that best describes their company.

The challenge with some competency frameworks is that they can be very broad and therefore do not provide guidance but rather can be perceived as a tick-box exercise. Additionally, these frameworks are sometimes applied in one human capital function such as performance management but not utilised in recruitment or training and development and therefore are not fully embraced.

If the competency framework is not tied to back to all human capital endeavours, it impacts the organisation at different touchpoints of the talent lifecycle, in attempting to build the workforce of the future. For example, if your competency framework does not link into your recruitment process then you may not bring in individuals based on what you are trying to build internally, potentially resulting in decreased cultural and behavioural alignment. If you are recruiting using a competency framework but linking the framework back into internal development, it may appear to candidates that you have guiding principles to find talent, but you are less focused on developing your talent. And if you bring in a competency framework in the performance management process, it may appear as though you are looking for behaviours to rate people against, but you are less focused on bringing in candidates who are more aligned to them and less focused on developing people internally to ensure they are set up for success based on the criteria outlined in the framework.

Once your competency framework is in place you need to decide at what stages in the talent lifecycle you want to implement these and how you are going to assess them. For example, at the recruitment stage, you may do a pre-screening call, personality assessment, aptitude assessment, technical test and structured interview all linked back to the requirements set out in the job description which will be based on the competency framework. When a new employee joins, you might use the assessment data obtained to generate a customised personal development plan for that individual. When conducting performance management, it may be useful to talk back to the competencies or job description in terms of which the employee was hired. After performance management, you might gather all the data to determine what training initiatives the learning and development team can focus on as you would have the data linked back to common themes. When determining who forms part of your talent pool, succession plans, and 9 box grids, consider all the data you have gathered from hire to date to inform your talent's next steps. And finally, when the employee leaves the organisation, is your exit interview based on the same set of competencies?

Pulling through the competency framework as a common thread allows all of your talent management initiatives to interlink, as they should, also providing you with data points to inform each talent management initiative, and longitudinal data to perform talent analytics when you have enough data.

After defining the roles and the overarching framework, you then need to consider which valid and reliable psychometric or non-psychometric assessments will form the foundation upon how you are going to successfully and objectively measure behaviours, aptitudes, technical skills and/or values expected of individuals related to the talent initiatives you are looking to inform.

This is how you build a workforce for today and tomorrow. But without shifting your mindset from the notion that people are assets to a talent mindset you are going to struggle to attract, develop and retain talent in your organisation.

Table 2: Shift in Mindset – Old to New*

Old Mindset About People	New Talent Mindset
A vague notion that "people are our most important asset".	A deep conviction that better talent leads to better corporate performance.
HR is responsible for people management.	All managers are accountable for strengthening their talent pool.
We have a two-day succession planning exercise once a year.	Talent management is a central part of how we run the company.
I work with people I inherit.	I take bold actions to build the talent pool I need.

*Adapted from *Harvard Business Review*[28]

Summary

Summary of chapter 1

1. The war for talent is still going on today, 21 years after the release of the publication (*The War for Talent*) which reminded employers of the need to strategically focus on talent development as a key-critical business priority.

2. AI is going to impact on the workplace – you need to ensure your company is ready by redefining job roles and realigning talent strategy to build out the critical skills required for the future in line with a competency framework which links into all aspects of the talent management process from hire to retire.

3. It's not just about talent management principles but building out a talent mindset in building the workforce with the right roles, the right competency framework and the appropriate assessments to set the business up for success.

Suggested Reads:

The War for Talent – *The McKinsey Quarterly* http://www.executivesondemand.net/managementsourcing/images/stories/artigos_pdf/gestao/The_war_for_talent.pdf

War for Talent – *Harvard Business Review* https://hbswk.hbs.edu/archive/war-for-talent

Chapter 2

The business case for utilising assessments

> **THIS CHAPTER COVERS:**
>
> - The costs of poor hiring decisions and employee attrition
> - Assessments embedded in the talent management model

The costs of poor hiring decisions and employee attrition

First recorded around 1530, the word "assessment" refers to the gathering of information to make an informed decision with regard to an internal or external candidate. The word "assessment" can also refer to the actual tool being utilised to assess a candidate. The assessment tools used to appraise or evaluate individuals have evolved over the years, with a focus shifting towards data collection, analytics, and artificial intelligence. The rise in technology has made these tools much more accessible and convenient now that they have become available online. Whilst most people associate the term "assessment" with selection, assessments are also utilised by organisations for developmental and performance purposes throughout the talent lifecycle.

As we have seen in chapter 1, the use of assessments has increased over time as talent management has become increasingly important in determining business success.

The use of assessments is extremely valuable when used by companies to ensure that they are putting the right people with the right capabilities, in the right jobs at the right time. This could be for recruitment or development purposes, but either way, the eye-opening costs associated with losing talent have been reported from various sources across the globe.

The key purpose of assessments is to increase the probability of hiring the best suited candidate who will fit into the company's culture and perform well in the role.

The costs associated with a bad hire depend on the job. However, they tend to be unexpectedly high. Some examples include:

In the United States (US):

- The Philadelphia Police, considered a small employer (5000 employees) could have saved $18 million a year by using assessment methods to select talent.[29]

- At the time (the 1980s) the US Government (4 million employees) could have saved $16 billion a year.[30]

- The American Management Association estimated that poor hiring decisions can cost companies 1.4 times an employee's annual salary.[31]

- The California Strategic HR Partnership calculated that for some positions the cost of a poor hiring decision can be almost ten times the employee's annual salary.[32]

In the United Kingdom (UK):[33]

- A cost of 16% of an employee's annual salary is estimated for high-turnover, low-paying jobs (employees earning under £30,000 a year). For example, the cost to replace a £10/hour retail employee would be £3,328.

- A cost of 20% of an employee's annual salary is estimated for midrange positions (employees earning £30,000 to £50,000 a year). For example, the cost to replace a £40,000 per annum manager would be £8,000.

- A cost of up to 213% of an employee's annual salary is estimated for highly educated, executive positions. For example, the cost to replace a £100,000 per annum CEO is £213,000.

> If you want one year of prosperity, grow grain, if you want ten years of prosperity, grow trees, if you want a hundred years of prosperity, grow people. — *Old Chinese proverb*

In countries like South Africa, things are no different as the costs for a bad hire are estimated to be around R325,000 (approx. $25,000) per employee.[34]

Behind these high figures are some of the obvious costs which include advertising, recruiting, training and the development of new employees. However, there are other costs involved such as lost business, opportunity costs and low performance until new hires are fully trained, the negative impact on morale, interview time taken up by HR and business people, agency fees in excess of 15% of a candidate's annual salary and these are just a few. It may be more useful to look at an example of the costs broken down.

A report carried out by Oxford Economics revealed that it costs a company over £30,000 to replace a member of staff. This figure is based on two main factors – firstly the cost of lost output (while the new employee is being upskilled) and secondly the logistical costs associated with recruiting and selecting a new employee.[35] The study also revealed that a new employee requires around 28 weeks to get to their optimum productivity level which has an associated cost of £25,181 per employee.[36] The logistical costs include:

Temporary replacement for the role before the new hire starts:	£3,618
Approximate management time spent to interview:	£767
Recruitment agency fees:	£454
Advertising the new role:	£398
HR time spent processing replacement:	£196

All the costs above amount to £30,614 (approx. $37,000 or approx. R529,164). The costs may be higher based on the role, the level, the scarcity of skills, the available talent and the additional time put in that is not accounted for in the calculations above.

Therefore, as can be viewed in the examples above, the costs of bad hiring choices and the expenses associated with losing an employee are massive and any endeavours that are undertaken to achieve better alignment between candidates and the company to make good hiring decisions and increase tenure will have an exponential financial benefit to the organisation. One way of doing this is through utilising the right assessments, throughout the talent management process, as this offers organisations huge financial benefits when the assessments are bringing in candidates who are adding value to your organisation. It may be very difficult to understand some of the intrinsic qualities of an individual through interviewing alone, and therefore if you can understand a potential employee in more depth before hiring them, why not pay a little more to go a long way. The above statistics report on losing employees in general but imagine the costs associated with losing talented employees.

Doug Conant, CEO of Campbell's Soup, once said: "To win in the marketplace you must first win in the workplace."

Assessments embedded in the talent management model

Talent management is simply defined as the recruitment, development, and retention of individuals who consistently deliver superior performance in the workplace. Through each of these activities, individuals can be assessed using both psychometric and non-psychometric assessments.

Assessments are no longer instruments utilised for recruitment purposes only. A study across 14 countries showed that the majority (94%) of organisations who used assessments, particularly psychometric assessments, did so during the hiring stage.[37] However, there has been a massive increase in the use of assessments, particularly psychometric assessments, not for recruitment but for internal purposes, which were reported at 43% of organisations in 2010 compared to 63% in 2016.[38] Also, the confidence which businesses have in the ability of these assessments in making more reliable and less risky decisions is up from 67% in 2010 to 81% in 2016.[39] These trends align with the history of talent development and the war for talent as companies are not just bringing in talent but also focus on retaining talented employees too.

The percentage of employers who believed that psychometric testing can predict future performance rose from under half (49%) in 2010 to 57% around 2016, illustrating that businesses are increasingly seeing the value that assessments bring to talent management.[40]

When looking at each of the stages of talent management, also known as the talent lifecycle, we know this model changes slightly depending on the author of the model. If we consider the model as it is below, there are various opportunities to bring in both psychometric and non-psychometric assessments and to conduct research to inform talent initiatives, a few of which have been noted on the following page.

Figure 5: Talent Lifecyle

The use of assessments at different stages of the talent management lifecycle:

Recruitment

- Biographical questionnaires
- Pre-screening solutions online, via phone or paper-and-pencil
- Culture-fit surveys
- Technical tests and other non-psychometric assessments
- Psychometric assessments
- Assessment centres

Selection

- Personality, values and aptitude assessments as well as other psychometric assessments
- Situational judgement tests
- Person–job matches
- Interviews

Training and Development

- Development centres
- Psychometric assessments and performance data to inform performance development plans and talent identification
- Team reports on psychometric assessments
- 360 assessments
- Integration projects
- Employee engagement surveys
- Employee wellbeing surveys
- Required training interventions
- Effectiveness of training interventions
- Career planning

Performance Management

- Skills audits
- 360 assessments

Succession Planning

- Potential and performance data from the psychometric assessments already run
- Person–job matches

Workforce Planning

- Data from HR, performance data, psychometric and non-psychometric assessment data

- Critical role identification

Summary of chapter 2

1. Poor hiring decisions across the globe are costing organisations a great deal of money; hence the need for objective assessment practices to assist in the selection process.

2. When assessing the impact or cost that is incurred when hiring candidates who are not a good fit for the role, we might not take into consideration some of the hidden costs which still affect the bottom-line.

3. Assessments are being used for selection but also have become increasingly popular for internal development.

Chapter 3

Assessments around the globe

> **THIS CHAPTER COVERS:**
>
> ■ Rules and regulations
>
> ■ The use of assessments as a human resource practitioner

Rules and regulations

In today's VUCA world, a company's success or failure will depend very much on the quality of its staff complement. Talent assessment is expanding across the globe, with some tests gaining more attention than others. Despite the increase in the use of assessments, psychometric and non-psychometric, only some countries have developed guidelines as well as legislation which define the use of these assessments. When searching for best practice on psychometric assessments, it may be difficult to find information about their use across different countries except for South Africa, the United Kingdom, and America. Some countries are less in favour of the use of psychometric assessments, particularly for selection purposes.

South Africa is known to have extremely strict guidelines as proposed by the Health Professions Council of South Africa (HPCSA), but the guidelines are also related to different forms of South African legislation such as the Labour Relations Act, the Employment Equity Act, and the Equality Act, to ensure that assessments are reliable, valid, utilised fairly, not biased and do not discriminate against any group.

Additionally, it is prescribed that individuals who administer, interpret and provide feedback on psychometric assessments are sufficiently qualified, accredited and experienced to provide such services.

Many countries will have legislation preventing discrimination but South Africa is known to have particularly inclusive legislation which prohibits discrimination based on race, gender, sex, pregnancy, family responsibility or status, marital status, ethnic or social origin, HIV/AIDS status, colour, sexual orientation, age, disability, religion, conscience, belief, culture, language and birth.

The United Kingdom also has regulatory bodies to provide guidelines for psychometric assessments namely the British Psychological Society (BPS) and the Health and Care Professions Council (HCPC) to govern the use of psychometrics and the registration of users to utilise psychometric assessments. The supporting legislation preventing discrimination on protected characteristics such as age, gender, race, religion, disability, sex, marriage and civil partnership, maternity and pregnancy is the Equality Act of 2010.

The United States has the American Psychological Association (APA) who are leaders in the realm of psychological testing and therefore have published guidelines that guide the development and use of psychological assessments. The Civil Rights Act of 1964 prevents the discrimination of employees based on sex, race, colour, national origin and religion.

All guidelines and legislation of the respective countries must be considered and observed when developing and implementing assessments into employment practices.

The use of assessments as an HR practitioner

The HR department encompasses a series of systems, policies and practices that help to assess, manage, support, train and sustain the workforce. As an HR practitioner, your focus is on people: how they fit into the job, into the company, and especially how they can be most effective in achieving high levels of performance. The increased use of assessments requires constant review and revision of processes, job profiles and competency frameworks as well as consideration of best practices when developing and selecting an assessment for recruitment or development purposes. These chapters provide greater insight into the types, development and use of assessments in the workplace.

As an HR practitioner, part of your role in the assessment process is to ensure that reliable, valid and non-biased assessments form part of your selection and development processes. Also, it is important to manage the data obtained through assessments as well as manage the feedback process which candidates go through. To this end, you are responsible for ensuring that all candidates (internal or external) go through the same process when completing assessments. If in doubt refer to the assessment providers of the assessments that you utilise.

With the rise of AI and the shift to build, buy, borrow or bot – the role of HR is becomingly increasingly more strategic.

The role of psychologists in the workplace

The psychologist in the workplace, also known as organisational, industrial, occupational or business psychologist, focuses on the dynamics at an individual, group and organisational level and they use research, theories and assessment techniques to identify issues and offer solutions with the aim of improving the well-being of employees and increasing performance in a company.

Success in the workplace is closely related to a company's ability to identify all the "gaps" in communication, leadership, decision making, team interaction, and so on. A psychologist is a trained individual able to analyse, design and implement various solutions to help solve individuals' and organisational problems like training needs analysis, attrition rate, motivation in employees, coaching leaders, analyses of leadership styles and checking their impact on employees' performance, formulating and implementing training programmes, carrying out psychometric testing for talent assessment, and so on. Their education teaches them about the science of human behaviour in the workplace and they possess deep knowledge about critical issues that affect the success in a company.

The psychological assessments encompass various types of data and multiple types of assessment such as behavioural observation, psychological tests, different types of interviews, questionnaires, rating scales, competency matrixes, and so on. Psychologists are trained to deal with the above professionally and ethically and can administer, interpret and provide feedback on psychometric assessments as well as non-psychometric assessments like competency-based interviews. They also conclude the assessments based on the data gathered from various sources and will effectively communicate the results both in verbal and written form. These chapters contain information that may already be available or known to psychologists but serve as refreshers on some of the topics covered.

Summary of chapter 3

1. There are different governing bodies, as well as legislation, to guide the development and use of assessments in the workplace.

2. All guidelines and legislation of the respective countries must be considered and observed when developing and implementing assessments into employment practices.

3. If you are unsure of the guidelines and legislation, contact a subject matter expert to guide best practice within your organisation.

Chapter 4

An overview of the different types of assessments

> **THIS CHAPTER COVERS:**
>
> ■ Overview of psychometric and non-psychometric assessments
>
> ■ Assessment techniques

Overview of psychometric and non-psychometric assessments

In the workplace, assessments can be classified into two groups:

■ Psychometric assessments and

■ Non-psychometric assessments

In determining whether an assessment is psychometric or non-psychometric, there are a few aspects to consider. An easy rule of thumb is to ask yourself if the construct in question is tangible. For example, can you see a person's personality? The answer is no. Some may argue that you can see personality by the behaviours people are engaged in, however, the behaviour stemming from personality is not a measure of personality itself, but rather a manifestation of personality.

Psychometrics not only measure constructs that are said to be less tangible, but they are also governed more strictly, in line with the psychometric properties which define them. In some countries psychometric assessments can only be administrated and interpreted by individuals who have studied for several years, written a board exam and undergone specific training on the psychometric they wish to utilise, while in other countries guidelines are less strict, suggesting that upskilling on the assessment is sufficient (as discussed in chapter 3).

The increased use of assessments has also led companies to develop their own psychometric and non-psychometric instruments, for internal use and consulting purposes. Because there are many different assessment providers, it is critical to ensure that the assessments you utilise are not discriminatory, are not biased, and are objective and reliable as well as valid.

In some instances, the assessments utilised particularly for selection purposes may need to be registered with a governing body. One such body in South Africa is the Health Professions Council of South Africa (HPCSA) while the British Psychological Society (BPS) is a governing body in the United Kingdom.

Before choosing assessments, it may be wise to consider some of the following factors:

- Constructs/skills/abilities you want to assess.
- The other determinants contributing to the decision-making process.
- Seniority/level of the position.
- Degree to which managerial/leadership ability is critical to success.
- Degree to which technical competence is critical to success.
- Time and effort required to use the chosen technique/s, in proportion to the risk of poor selection.
- Available resources including time, budget and technology.
- Skills, knowledge, experience and qualifications of assessors.
- The impact the assessment will have on the candidate.

- The need to give feedback to candidates and the professionals who will do so.

As part of any selection or development process, assessments should not be the only determinant upon which decisions are made. A holistic view of the candidate is important in determining suitability for a role or for a training intervention. Some organisations are comfortable in developing selection and development processes and assigning particular assessments to various stages of the selection process, while other companies prefer to seek expert advice from organisational or occupational psychologists based on their particular scope of practice. If in doubt, rather refer to subject matter experts in the field such as specialised consultancies, psychometric assessment developers and providers, as well as governing bodies.

Assessment techniques

With various methods available and increased modes of delivery, organisations generally utilise a range of different techniques to assess candidates for selection and/or development purposes depending on the predefined selection process and based on the resources available. The below methods can be utilised for both psychometric and non-psychometric assessments.

Face-to-face methods

Face-to-face methods have been the main method of assessment for many years and have decreased to some degree with the introduction of new ways to administer assessments. Interviews (individual and panel), role-plays, psychometric assessments, assessment centres and other forms of assessment are moving towards methods that are less human-dependent.

Although it may be obvious, as companies are relying more heavily on technology, it is important to remember the impact of verbal and non-verbal cues during these interactions. Factors such as general posture, tone of voice, eye contact, hand gestures, facial expressions, distraction with your mobile phone (or laptop) and decreased attention, all impact on a candidate's level of interaction when being assessed. Despite the increase in the use of technology for assessment purposes, face-to-face methods will still be utilised somewhere along the selection process even if only for the final interview.

With an increase in globalisation, the increased war on talent and employees working across the globe, face-to-face methods may be costly, especially if you are interviewing a few candidates who need to be flown in from across the globe. In this instance, companies may rely solely on the use of technology.

Virtual methods

With the increase in the speed of the internet, as well as increased accessibility to the internet by the general population, human resource practitioners are taking advantage of the ability to conduct interviews, hold meetings and conduct assessments virtually either over the phone or through video calling. Virtual does not only refer to video but also calling and recording capabilities.

In some instances, organisations request individuals to submit a recording of themselves, usually consisting of answers to predefined questions or a topic that has been suggested beforehand. After the recordings have been submitted, they are reviewed and could be outsourced if a company chooses to use internal human resources for other activities.

Although virtual methods may be more convenient, you do have some disadvantages such as reliance on technology, potential decreased connection to the candidate due to a lack of human interaction, as well as missing out on verbal cues which you may not observe over video calling or through a phone call.

Online methods

Numerous assessments can be administered online in assessing the various skills or capabilities of a potential candidate. Most assessments nowadays are carried out online as assessments have been developed and tested using encrypted links to access the assessment instead of accessing the assessment via hard copy as can be observed in cases of multiple-choice questionnaires, essays, case studies, and other straightforward psychometric assessments.

Some of the more complex assessments are also being carried out online such as simulations, animations, tutorials, games, and assessment or development centres to name a few. One such assessment includes animated Situational Judgment Tests, which can be administered online instead of requiring candidates to attend assessment administration at the respective hiring organisation.

The ability to access assessments online has resulted in the rise in adaptive assessments which refers to assessments that adapt based on how you answer a particular question. This can also reduce the time it takes for candidates to complete the assessment as they may get to a particular skill level a lot quicker or demonstrate the required competency sooner than others.

One of the challenges which still exists to date, despite online psychometric assessments being available since 1996, is the need to verify the identity of the candidate completing the assessment. This is particularly important when assessing candidates using aptitude and technical assessments for selection purposes because candidates could ask someone else to complete the assessment for them. Test developers have implemented a variety of different solutions to this such as re-testing individuals when they attend an interview. However, a standard practice is yet to be developed.

Artificial Intelligence

As the buzz word in many sectors and industries, artificial intelligence has also been incorporated into assessments and selection processes across the globe. Everyone knows that AI is coming but not many understand what is it and the impact it will have.

AI was introduced to assessments in the 1990s when paper-based methods shifted to computer-based ones. Chatbot-type conversations in situational judgement testing, algorithm-based decisions and gamification methods are becoming more common in the assessment space. There are different AI processes which inform assessments which include:

Robotic process automation refers to a preconfigured software module that uses a set of predefined instructions to automate rule-based tasks. This kind of system cannot learn and requires structured data. Some may classify this type of artificial intelligence as automation instead of AI.

Pattern matching refers to a system being able to recognise a sequence of responses by a candidate. This AI technique is often used to identify emotions.

Natural language processing refers to the use of text and speech analytics to extract the underlying meaning and can be used in analysing speech in interview question responses.

With some of the applications mentioned above, AI has the power to analyse and interpret large amounts of candidate data which previously required many human-hours.

Some benefits of AI include:

- Increased accuracy
- Increased objectivity
- Reduced bias
- Consistent administration
- Highly interactive

Artificial intelligence is not without some disadvantages, some of which include the lack of human interaction, potentially ruling out candidates who bring something different to what you may have been assessing for. It may also result in very similar candidates being selected, thus decreasing diversity in thought, and lastly may rule out talented candidates who do not have internet access and may be more difficult to adapt to the needs of candidates with disabilities.

One of the controversial AI-driven assessment techniques includes social media profile and presence scanning. Some argue that this kind of assessment breaches candidate privacy and leaves candidates with a bad impression of companies that utilise this kind of assessment in their screening process.

Now that the different methods and techniques for administering assessments have been discussed, let's look at the different types of psychometric and non-psychometric assessments that exist.

Summary of chapter 4

1. There are a variety of both psychometric and non-psychometric assessments for use in selection and development initiatives, which can be administered using multiple different techniques.

2. There is a difference between automation and AI.

3. AI is becoming increasingly popular in the selection process.

Chapter 5

Psychometric assessments

> **THIS CHAPTER COVERS:**
>
> ■ Types of psychometric assessments
>
> ■ Development of psychometric assessments
>
> ■ Reliability
>
> ■ Validity
>
> ■ Considering fairness and bias
>
> ■ Understanding norms
>
> ■ Maintaining ethical standards

Types of psychometric assessments

Psychometrics is the field of study concerned with the theory and technique of psychological measurement and/or talent assessment in an objective and empirical manner using a variety of different instruments and methods.

There are a variety of different tests available by different providers depending on what you are looking to assess as being relevant to the role you are assessing for. Listed below are some of the assessments available in no particular order.

Intelligence tests involve a series of tasks that measure an individual's capacity to learn, to make abstractions or to deal with new situations. Intelligence can be split into fluid intelligence, which refers to an individual's ability to deal with new situations without previous knowledge, and crystallised intelligence, which is an individual's ability to use experience to solve problems. Intelligence tests typically measure a construct called IQ (intelligence quotient), 'g' (general intelligence) or an individual's intelligence quotient rather than specific skill sets. The use of intelligence tests has historically been controversial as they have been suggested to be biased based on environmental factors such as educational background which impacts on cultural differences. Examples of commonly used intelligence tests include the Stanford-Binet Intelligence Scale and some which claim to be culturally fair such as Cattell's Culture-fair Intelligence Test to name a few.

Aptitude tests assess a candidate's ability to work with particular information including verbal, numerical, error-checking, diagrammatic, spatial, mechanical and abstract information. Many of these tests will be short and timed to assess the candidate's test performance under pressure. The test will usually have right or wrong answers associated with them or differing levels of correctness. Examples of some common aptitude tests include Mental Agility Profiler (MAP), Swift Aptitude range and the General Reasoning Test.

Personality tests assess an individual's personality constructs as typically defined by the five-factor personality model and variations which stem from this. Personality theory suggests that personality can be trait-like or state-like. Trait-based personality refers to longer-term characteristics that individuals are suggested to exhibit while state-based personality refers to more flexible capabilities that change over time. These kinds of assessments are usually self-report, untimed and result in personality profiles that are not necessarily right or wrong but rather more or less of a fit based on the requirements of the role. Some examples of personality assessments include PsyCap Potential, Saville Wave and the 16PF.

"Over 85% of Fortune 500 companies are using psychometric testing as one of the initial stages of recruiting."[41]

Emotional Intelligence tests generally assess an individual's ability to empathise with others, understand own and others' emotions and adapt accordingly. Some assessments claim to assess EQ (emotional quotient), which has been suggested to decrease as IQ increases, while others look at the skills of individuals to understand, reflect and adapt to their own and others' emotions. EQ assessments are generally self-report, not timed and result in a profile being generated based on an individual's responses. Again, there are no wrong or right answers, but some roles may require a certain level of emotional awareness and adaptability to respond appropriately to colleagues and clients. Some examples of emotional intelligence tests include the EQ-I.

Situational judgement tests (SJTs) assess a candidate's ability to choose the most appropriate action in the workplace aligned with the organisation's culture. The tests are developed as either a static or animated assessment which creates a common work scenario that a candidate may be faced with on the job. Usually, SJTs will be based on a specific job function, or context, such as administration, customer service, consulting and conflict resolution and can be industry-specific too, depending on the level of customisation. Candidates are then required to respond to the assessment as they would on any given day at work, with several different response choices available. The answers are usually graded on the level of correctness.

Motivation tests assess a candidate's intrinsic and extrinsic motivation behind their behaviour. Some intrinsic motivators include meaningful work, task variety, challenging work, recognition, learning something new and some extrinsic motivators include salary, benefits, awards and winning.

Other workplace assessments include the assessment of employee engagement, job satisfaction, counterproductive workplace behaviours, perceived insider status, perceived organisational support and integrity.

Development of psychometric assessments

Developing psychometric assessments requires a great deal of research in conjunction with expert consultation, statistical analyses, and continuous refinement. Some organisations will embark on creating in-house assessments to utilise for recruitment and development purposes. However, most organisations make use of existing assessments from credible assessment providers and accredited consulting firms.

The general process of assessment development is described below using the example of assessing humility for demonstration purposes. This in no way includes the details of carrying out psychometric assessment development but rather provides an overview to provide psychometric users with an understanding of the general process.

General assessment development process:

1. Decide on what you want to measure, for example, humility.

2. Identify if there is a gap in the market and determine if the market, and what the market, would pay for the proposed assessment.

3. Conduct research into understanding the theoretical foundation of the assessment and the construct you are looking to measure and whether sub-factors make up the construct. For example, are you just looking at humility or is humility made up of sub-factors like honesty, consistency, and empathy? If your research shows varied models and differing views, then you can confirm which theory is most appropriate when you do the statistical analyses, but you still need to put a peg in the ground as this will inform your item development.

4. Start developing and creating items to form part of the assessment. You need to create more items than you expect to utilise in your assessment because some of your items may not show statistical significance or sufficient association with the construct and therefore as you remove items later on, you don't want to have to utilise a different sample. For example, if you decided to assess humility as a single factor then you would create items linking to it. If you chose to look at humility as defined by three sub-factors then you would need to create items for each of the sub-factors instead of the main factor alone. If you are planning to have 10 items for each sub-factor then aim to create at least 20 test items per sub-factor.

5. Check and cross-check that your items make logical sense in terms of research and existing measures (if applicable). Decide on the response format (for example, Likert-type, multiple-choice, true or false) and the means of administration (for example, paper-and-pencil, online or using an app).

6. Decide on how you are going to administer the assessment and to which audience, as an initial pilot, to get a sense of the look and feel of the items and duration of the assessment. It needs to be made very clear to participants that the assessment is being trialled and there are various guidelines that need to be incorporated such as anonymity, confidentiality, informed consent and voluntary participation, some of which are covered later in this chapter under ethics.

7. Upon completion and feedback from test participants regarding the usability of the assessment, you may want to make some refinements and revisions to some of the items, after which you can administer your assessment to a larger sample. When determining a sample keep in mind that the sample needs to be large enough to be able to run certain statistics and the sample needs to be diverse enough to be generalisable. Most statistical techniques prescribe minimum and ideal sample sizes.

8. After collecting data through your larger sample you can begin to run some statistics depending on the type of data you have collected but generally factor analyses and structural equation modelling are statistical techniques utilised in assessment development to determine which items are loading onto which factors, how many factors are making up your constructs and which items need to be revised or removed.

9. Use the statistical analyses and your research to confirm if the item loadings make sense loaded on their respective factors. For example, if you went with the three sub-factors making up humility, namely honesty, consistency and empathy, an item which says "I share my views even if they negatively impact others" should theoretically and logically be loaded under honesty or consistency and less so under empathy but if, through the statistical analysis, it does load under empathy, you may need to remove the item.

10. After refining, removing and adjusting items, re-run your statistics to determine if the items and model work better, which will be followed by other statistics and expert guidance to determine the reliability and validity of the assessment, the scoring and norm groups to ultimately write-up the technical manual.

11. In some instances, even expert assessment developers may outsource their statistics and validation studies to further show objectivity.

12. When the assessment has been deemed suitable to use in the public domain, you can begin to develop your go-to-market strategy including accreditation and marketing material.

Reliability

The concept of reliability refers to the stability of a construct to remain relatively unchanged and produce similar results when re-assessed over time. This can be assessed through several methods namely through measuring the Cronbach Alpha, Split-half reliability,

Test-retest and Alternative form reliability of assessments. First, it is important to understand the premise behind test reliability known as Classical Test Theory.

Classical Test Theory is a body of psychometric research that predicts the outcomes of psychological testing. It suggests that for each candidate that participates in a psychometric assessment their results are made up of three components. The first component is the observed score, which is the resulting score from completing the assessment (true score combined with random error). The second component is the true score, which is the theoretical score that candidates would score if there was no room for error. We know that this is not possible due to the infinite amount of circumstances that may impact a candidate, some of which are within our control and others which are not, which result in incremental amounts of error, which is the third component.

We aim to reduce error as much as possible and as we do this through methods such as standardised testing conditions, the reliability of the test increases. Higher test reliability would yield more accurate true scores. The lower the error, the more accurately the results will be impacting positively on the confidence in using the results for selection and/or development purposes.

For example, if we weigh each apple from a bag of apples and get an average weight of 100 grams with a standard error of 20 grams, that is a large variance between 120 grams and 80 grams. We might be hesitant to include in our advertising that the apples are approximately 100 grams each. After reassessing the apples we notice that some apples are more shrivelled than others (picked at different times), some apples have stems attached while others do not, some stems are larger than others that also have stems and some apples are wet after being washed. Therefore, all four of those factors were contributing to the difference in measurements to some degree. After ensuring that apples were weighed directly after picking, were dried after being washed and all stems were removed, we still had an average of 100 grams, however the standard error reduced to 10 grams. We now have variance from 90 grams to 110 grams which is much less and we can say with more confidence that each apple weighs approximately 100 grams. The standard error of 10 grams may be due to some aspects we haven't thought of, or factors outside of our control such as quality of the soil impacting on the growth of the apples, the amount of water they receive throughout their growth, amount of sunlight they receive, etc.

When looking at the different types of reliability there are four common types to consider:

1. **Cronbach Alpha** – A measure of internal consistency indicating how closely the items of the scale or scales relate to each other. A higher score is more favourable with scores ranging from 0 to 1. Scores closer to 1 suggest higher levels of internal consistency with an ideal score above 0.70. This suggests that the items of a scale are closely related and measure the same construct. A score of 1 may mean that your items are all asking the same thing too similarly and therefore you may remove or alter some of the items.

2. **Split-half reliability** – Also a measure of internal consistency, which measures the extent to which all parts contribute equally to what is being measured. This is done by randomly splitting the test into two separate halves and comparing the results of each group. These results are then used to remove or alter items under each of the halves.

3. **Test-retest reliability** – This reliability technique refers to the stability of the measurement to remain unchanged over time and is considered a form of external reliability. It involves testing at one time and conducting the same test again at a different time and comparing the results. The timing is important because if you retest too quickly, candidates may use memory recall to replicate the same results. However, if you leave it for too long before you retest, candidates may have changed.

4. **Alternate or parallel form reliability** – This measure of reliability refers to the congruence of scores obtained by

completing one version of the test and completing a different version of the test at a different time.

By assessing the reliability of an assessment, you answer some of the following questions:

- Is the assessment producing accurate results?
- Do different items measure the same construct?
- How stable are scores over time?
- Are there aspects of the assessment that might bring a different conclusion when completing it again tomorrow?
- Do the different forms of the test measure the same ability?

An assessment can be reliable but that does not mean it is valid. However, an assessment cannot be valid if it is unreliable. Reliability is necessary, but not sufficient, for validity.

Validity

Validity refers to the degree to which an instrument assesses what it claims to measure.

There are several different forms of validity, some of which can be assessed through statistical techniques and others through user feedback and expert consultation:

1. **Construct validity** – A measure has construct validity if it is related to the theoretical construct/s which it claims to measure, which can be supported by evidence, theory, and similarity to other instruments that measure the same construct. This can be assessed qualitatively by attempting to explain the results obtained on the assessment by theory, or other evidence, and comparing the content of the items to existing theory. Construct validity can be confirmed quantitatively by comparing the results of the assessment in question to other assessments that claim to measure the same construct.

2. **Content validity** – A measure of validity determining the degree to which an assessment measures the full dimension of what it claims to measure, including the purpose of the assessment. For example, asking someone to complete a maths test for a role in creative writing suggests that the test has no content validity because you want to assess aspects relevant to the role, which in this case is not maths ability. If we look at a more complex example, if you provide a numerical reasoning test for an accounting clerk position, the test may not cover the full range of responsibilities that the successful incumbent would be required to do, however, it assesses a major skill required for the role and therefore it has moderate to high content validity.

3. **Face validity** – This measure of validity provides the degree to which respondents, reviewers, and administrators believe the items of the assessment are relevant to the purpose of the assessment and the construct it claims to measure.

4. **Faith validity** – In assessing whether an instrument measures what it claims to, faith validity refers to the degree to which participants, administrators, and reviewers believe that the assessment is valid.

5. **Criterion-related validity** – This form of validity refers to the ability of a measure to predict outcome variables or a particular criterion. There are two types of criterion-related validity, defined by the time at which the data is collected and the subsequent use of the data, to estimate what outcomes one expects to see. **Concurrent validity** refers to the comparison (correlation) between the assessment data and outcome data being collected at the same time. **Predictive validity** refers to the assessment data being collected before the outcome data and running analyses to determine the predictability of the assessment data in predicting outcomes such as job satisfaction, job performance, promotability, potential and tenure.

6. **Consequential validity** – The degree to which an instrument brings about positive or negative consequences. For example, negative consequential validity would be someone scoring

highly on language proficiency, then practising less because of this, which then leads to decreased language proficiency. Positive consequential validity is when someone obtains a high score on the assessment, resulting in the individual teaching other people to learn a language due to their increased confidence in their language proficiency.

Assessments which are reliable and valid are more defensible as they provide an audit trail of the necessary qualitative and quantitative steps needed to ensure that the assessment is accurate in what it measures and it is, in fact, measuring what it claims to. These are not the only considerations in determining whether an assessment is ready to be utilised.

Many assessment developers, psychologists and practitioners are also tasked to ensure that assessments are fair and not biased in any way.

Considering fairness and bias

Test fairness refers to the equitable treatment of all participants who complete an assessment in reference to test design, test administration, scoring and feedback without any undue influence from other irrelevant variables. Tests that fail to meet the criteria of fairness will show score differences for predefined groups of examinees, and this quantitative difference is referred to as bias. Bias is a non-random (systematic) error that represents the quantitative evidence that supports lack of fairness of a certain psychometric test in relation to a particular group of people. Anyone working with assessment data, psychometric or non-psychometric, has a duty of care to ensure that fairness is applied to all participants throughout assessment processes.

In some instances, individuals with disabilities may not be able to complete some assessments in their current form or at all. Therefore, adjustments should be made to assist and cater to the needs of individuals who are less able to complete the assessment under general testing conditions but still meet the requirements of the role. An example includes an individual who is unable to view a computer screen at the zoom at which the test was designed to operate. In some instances, test publishers have adapted versions or have designed assessments that still function with the screen zoomed in.

Understanding norms

Many psychometric assessments do not use the raw (observed) score as the final score. Instead, to compare an individual's raw score to that of other people, the raw score is compared to norm tables to determine the individual's performance against a normal distribution, also known as normed scores. This allows us to present the data in many ways, but most importantly, it allows us to compare the individual's performance to that of other people who have also participated in taking the test.

Norms are standardised scores that represent an individual's performance compared to other people who have taken the test. When working with large amounts of data, it can be useful to represent the data using a few commonly understood statistical values which describe the data, such as the mean, median and mode – also known as measures of central tendency.

The mean refers to the average of the data. For example, if we have 6 scores of 15, 20, 20, 35, 40 and 45 the mean or average would be 29.17.

The median refers to data-point, which is in the middle of the data. If we use the same 6 scores above, the median would be 27.5 (as calculated by adding 20 to 35 and dividing by 2).

The mode refers to the number which appears the most, which would be the number 20 in the example above.

The mean is usually the most utilised measure of central tendency, especially when the data is normally distributed, which is determined through a variety of qualitative and quantitative methods. By using the definitions above and following the example below, they assist in describing the sample and the data, and allow you to understand how the data is 'spread' across a normal distribution. When scores have been standardised, they can be converted to stanines, stens or percentiles (to name a few) to describe the data as compared to the sample.

A few additional terms include:

The norm group refers to the sample of people who the candidate is being compared to. It is critical to ensure that the norm group is comprised of individuals who contribute to the type of sample you are trying to create. For example, it may be less useful to have a norm group consisting of scores obtained by students if you wish to compare the scores of a senior leader in a large company. You want to be able to say that the senior leader scored better than, the same as, or higher than other senior leaders.

The Normal distribution refers to the scores of the norm group being clustered around a single average score as represented by a normal bell curve graph. Approximately 68% of the population fall within 1 standard deviation on either side of the average (mean +1 standard deviation and the mean -1 standard deviation).

The Standard deviation shows how 'spread' the scores are, from the average across the norm group, and normal distribution. If you look at the standard deviation score of the data, a low standard deviation means that the scores are close together while a larger standard deviation suggests the scores are more spread out. Standard deviation can also be represented on a normal distribution, with the common classification of 1, 2, 3 or 4 standard deviations on either side of the mean to indicate where scores are positioned (as represented in the diagram on the following page).

Imagine that a basketball teacher is looking to determine whether a student is of sufficient height to nominate the student for the school basketball team. The teacher measures the student, who is 1.90m in height. This is only a number which we would call raw data, as no transformations have been undertaken to the data. The teacher then decides to use the other players as a comparison and measures their heights. The measurements vary; however, the scores tend to be clustered around a height of 1.81m. So, this is the average of the scores (the mean). Since the first student was 1.90m, when compared to 1.81m, we would say that the student is taller than the average. If we had to plot the student on a normal distribution, the student would be above the 50th percentile. It would be less useful to just use the student's score without a comparison.

Below is a diagram of a normal distribution bell curve with some of the labels as mentioned above.

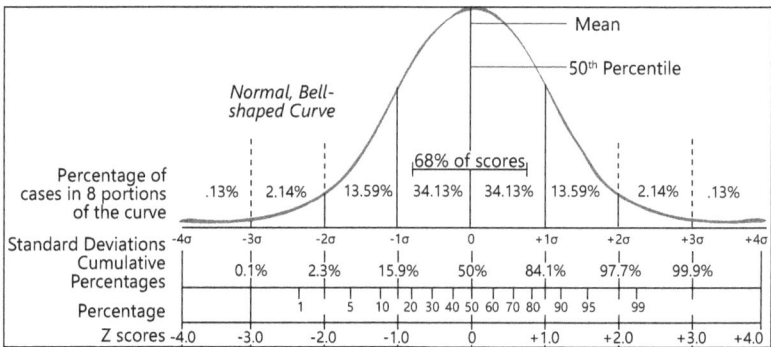

Figure 6: Normal Distribution Bell Curve

There is a lot more information relating to norms, norm tables, and normal distribution. Therefore it would be useful to do additional reading if you would like to understand these concepts in more detail.

Maintaining ethical standards

As mentioned, the HPCSA and the BPS have provided ethical guidelines relating to the countries in which the bodies govern. However, there are common ethical guidelines that do not relate to the use of assessments alone but the general ethical use of data, assessments and feedback to candidates. The information below in no way supersedes or replaces country-specific guidelines and legislation and can be used as an additional source of information only. If in doubt refer to assessment specialists.

1. **Informed Consent**

   Provide candidates with enough information to determine whether they want to be part of a particular process. In recruitment, this is sometimes assumed when candidates are applying for a role because in applying for a position, they are providing consent to be involved in the selection process. However, it is important to outline the process for candidates to decide whether they want to be part of it. It becomes increasingly important for internal processes as well, as some candidates may not be aware of potential negative outcomes associated with development processes, and should be made aware of these to inform their decision to be involved or not.

2. **Confidentiality**

   This involves advising the candidate before taking a test where and/or how their data will be stored, those who will have access to the data and what the data will be used for. During feedback sessions, this refers to the conversations that are had in the session, which can have exceptions to discuss some topics further with permission from the candidate. Personal and private information shared during these sessions is confidential.

3. **Professional Competence**

   The administrators of the tests, interpreters and those providing feedback need to be appropriately trained, upskilled and qualified to administer the assessment as well as interpret or provide feedback to others. There is also an ethical duty to maintain competence in the assessments you are working with to ensure you are up to date with the assessment being utilised and that you have the relevant experience in working with the assessment.

4. **Voluntary Participation**

   Individuals participating should not be coerced in any way. They should be able to opt-out of the process or the assessment at any stage should they not wish to proceed. Implications for choosing not to partake, participate or proceed should be outlined. For example, if a candidate is part of a process for a promotion and the candidate chooses not to complete a psychometric assessment that forms part of the selection process, then the candidate should be made aware that their application will not progress further.

5. **Professional Consultation**

As professionals we do our utmost to ensure that participants' information is kept confidential. Under exceptional circumstances, an incident may require the opinion of a second assessor or another qualified professional and therefore in some instances a professional may consult with another for guidance but must, by all means possible, keep the identity of the participant in question undisclosed.

6. **Proper Conditions and Appropriate Surroundings**

Tests or assessments should be conducted and completed in an environment that is quiet and free from distraction to allow test takers to perform optimally. Feedback provided to candidates or clients should be in an area where confidential and potentially sensitive information cannot be heard by others who are not authorised and should not be privy to the information.

Above we have discussed some of the best practice guidelines regarding ethics. However, every country has its own rules and legislation which must be observed and upheld.

Some of the guidelines below may have been discussed already, but to ensure best practice, the appropriate use of assessments and the correct storage of data, some additional guidelines include:

- Follow the administration, scoring and interpretation instructions contained in the manual of the instrument concerned.
- Ensure that the assessment is administered, scored and interpreted by a qualified and experienced professional.

- Access to psychometric tests and questionnaires should be restricted to administrators and test takers only.

- Indicate to participants how their data will be used, who it will be shared with and how long it will be stored.

- Maintain confidentiality and only share confidential information with legitimate cause and with the respondent's full knowledge.

- Observe all guidelines and legislation regarding the collection, storage, dissemination and destruction of data.

- Provide appropriate feedback on results and adequately explain the purpose, implications and the limitations of the psychometric instruments being utilised.

- Be aware of and mindful of any differences in the scores between groups, in particular, those of a different race, gender, ethnic background or who are disabled, in order to make accommodations or revisions where necessary.

Summary of chapter 5

1. There are a variety of different psychometric assessments that are utilised to measure different constructs in the selection and development process.

2. Developing assessments requires specific expertise, and a great amount of time and data to ensure that it is reliable, valid, fair, and unbiased.

3. It is critical to ensure ethical standards are maintained throughout the selection, development, feedback, and data storage process as outlined by your location, legislation and governing bodies.

Chapter 6

Non-psychometric assessments

Types of non-psychometric assessments

Let's have a look at those techniques included within the non-psychometric classification. These are tools that practitioners utilise in isolation, or in conjunction, with psychometric testing:

■ Informal meetings (also referred to as connect sessions).

■ Interviews (structured, unstructured, stress, behavioural & panel).

■ Work simulations (role-plays, presentations, vision-speeches, group discussions).

■ Technical tests.

■ Disclosure assessments (criminal record, credit checks, education checks and references).

Informal Meetings

The informal meeting or connect session seems to be increasing in popularity as individuals are building out their networks. Not only are potential employees seeking these meetings with potential employers, but employers are actively seeking out talented employees to set up connect sessions with, in order to build relationships and potentially bring that person across to their organisation when they are ready. Although this may not be a valid and reliable assessment technique, it seems to be increasingly popular as senior leaders are building out their networks and potential talent pools.

Interviews

Interviews have been utilised and trusted by businesses for a number of years, which is why it is not surprising to hear that interviews are widely used as a tool of assessment.

Structured Interviews

This type of interview is usually more formal and methodical and may be carried out by a single interviewer or multiple interviewers (referred to as panel interview). The first questions are typically "icebreakers", used to relax the candidate before the standardised and more formal questions are asked. After the interview, the candidate is scored on their responses to the predefined questions and their performance during the interview.

Unstructured Interviews

As the name implies, this can be an informal and emergent form of interview, with general questions about what the candidate is looking for, some background on the company and subsequent questions that may seem appropriate, which flow off the back of the conversation. This is more conversational, and employers tend to use this type of interview to make candidates feel more comfortable to share information relating to how they perform without feeling the need to impress the interviewers.

Stress Interviews

This type of interview is less common. However, it may be used by organisations that are aware that the role requires an individual who can perform well under pressure. The questions may be similar to those posed in a structured or unstructured interview. However, additional factors are usually incorporated into the process such as the interviewer appearing to be uninterested, the interviewer cutting the candidate off before they finish their response, asking the candidate difficult riddles and/or putting candidates under time pressure to answer difficult questions. Although there may appear to be some benefits to utilising this style of interviewing to get an idea of how a candidate may perform under pressure, there are also ethical considerations such as the potential impact or harm to an individual being interviewed as well as their experience of the organisation, which they may take away as being negative.

Behavioural Interviews

One of the widely used methods of job interviewing is competency-based or behavioural interviewing. The rationale behind this type of interview rests on the premise that past performance predicts future behaviour. Therefore, the questions are asked to explore how candidates have dealt with similar situations in the past, which they may face in the role for which they are applying. The structure of these interviews usually follows the STAR method – Situation, Task, Action, Result.

Panel interviews

This method involves more than one interviewer. Each of the methods above can be adapted to be in the form of a panel interview. Panel interviews are recommended in order to decrease subjectivity, potential bias or favouritism that a single interviewer may have towards a candidate: consciously or unconsciously. The concept of inter-rater reliability comes into question, which looks at the degree to which different interviewers' scores are aligned when evaluating the same candidate.

What exactly are interviews trying to assess?

In a study by Huffcutt and Colleagues,[42] a review of 47 studies was conducted to understand what the interviews aimed to measure. The results showed that the following constructs were assessed during interviews with a higher percentage indicating constructs that were most measured:

- 35% assessed personality dimensions
- 28% measured social skills
- 16% were aiming to assess general mental ability
- 10% focused on knowledge & skills
- 4% on interests
- 3% on organisational fit between the candidate and the company.

The results above illustrate that approximately 51% of constructs that interviewers assessed during the analysis of the 47 studies relate to constructs that are less tangible and difficult to assess through an interview, namely personality traits or dimensions, as well as general mental ability.

Methods to increase the reliability and validity of interviews:

- Standard process and approach when conducting interviews
- Standardised questions
- Standardised scoring legend indicating what great looks like
- The same interviewers are used
- Questions are based on workplace examples and are job-related
- Bias training for interviewers

Work Simulations

This assessment method not only gives employers an idea of what to expect from candidates when in the role, but it also gives candidates an idea of the types of tasks that they might be involved in should they join the company. There are many types of work simulations to include such as in-basket assessments, roleplays, presentations and vision speeches which can all be administered through pen-and-paper, online or face-to-face methods.

Work simulations allow hiring and line managers to evaluate candidates based on relevant tasks which are applicable to the role, giving them an indication of how candidates may perform in the role if they are successful in the selection process. Work simulations must be translated into observable tasks matched to the right role, and level, in order to see performance indicators or behavioural indicators that you expect a candidate to demonstrate.

Usually, work simulations form part of assessment centres, but it is not unheard of for some work simulation exercises to form part of a general selection process.

Technical Tests

These are generally related to skills that are required on the job and can be based on the use of software, general practices relating to a particular topic and general knowledge tests to get a sense of a candidate's general understanding of a particular area, industry or skillset. These consist of right and wrong answers and will usually be presented as a pass or fail and as a percentage. Examples include tests which assess a candidate's proficiency with Microsoft Office, Accounting software, graphic design software, basic accounting principles, legislation and even typing speed. Most of these assessments are administered online, with some being available using paper-and-pencil methods.

Disclosure Assessments

These assessments are generally carried out by recruitment agencies, however some organisations make this assumption and overlook these assessments altogether. These include background checks, references, criminal record screening, credit-score screening and educational background confirmation.

When conducting these tests or checks on a candidate, express written consent is required, with informed consent advising the candidate exactly what the results will be used for and some roles indicating that a "clear" record is a prerequisite to move forward in the selection process. For example, in some countries, it is not permitted for black-listed individuals with poor credit scores to work as financial advisers. Such tests can also involve alcohol and drug screening, which are particularly contentious, and legislation may vary depending on your geography.

A variety of assessments have been covered, including both psychometric and non-psychometric assessment methods. In bringing it all together, a combination of assessments can be used to create an assessment or development centre that provides an array of data-points to aid in decision-making.

Summary of chapter 6

1. Non-psychometric assessments are still utilised in selection and development processes today, with some methods proving to be more objective than others.

2. Some non-psychometric assessments attempt to measure psychometric constructs which may be better measured through psychometric assessments.

3. Assessment methods utilised need to relate back to the requirements of the job/role.

Chapter 7

An overview of assessment and development centres

....

> **THIS CHAPTER COVERS:**
>
> ■ A brief introduction to assessment and development centres and some general principles on how to create them.

Assessment centres (ACs) have been used since the mid-20th century and have a good track record in helping organisations to build a high-quality workforce. Assessment centres are referred to as the "premier" selection technique because they can be costly in terms of investment and time to develop, as well as administer, but are also effective in predicting suitability of a candidate for a role. Their effectiveness in predicting success in a job is said to justify the costs for many employers.

For many years, the interview was the key tool used by organisations in the recruitment and selection process, but studies of recruitment methodologies have shown that interviews are not a particularly accurate predictor of future job performance when used alone. Interviews rely on human evaluation of a candidate's performance, and as discussed can be influenced by bias.

....

Assessment Centres
....

Assessment centres consist of a combination of several different job-relevant assessments to increase the objectivity of the selection process as well as the reliability and validity of the results to predict job success. In addition, more than one assessor is utilised to assist in evaluating potential employees, making the process more objective. The organisation also assesses candidates on a range of exercises. The use of a variety of assessments not only increases the amount of data available to score candidates, but it also provides more opportunities for candidates to exhibit what the assessors are looking for. Some exercises may be completed alone, and other exercises in groups, while some assessment centres may be completely alone or completely group-oriented.

While psychometric assessments may bring to light the potential of a candidate, as well as less tangible constructs, the results obtained during an assessment centre provide an indication of a candidate's current performance.

General principles when developing an assessment centre:

- Put together a matrix of the skills, abilities, competencies, behaviours, etc (dimensions) relevant to the role, that you wish to assess and indicate how you are going to assess them.

- Prioritise the dimensions that are most critical to the role (maximum 8 dimensions).

- Determine if the assessment methods are feasible based on the time available (assessment centres can run from 2 hours to 8 hours).

- Each method/exercise should assess more than one dimension (3 to 5 dimensions each).

- Each dimension should be measured by more than one method.

- Assessments should be job-relevant.

- Detailed and explicit criteria for assessors is required.

- Evaluations should be transformed into scores based on predefined scoring criteria.

- A washup session should be conducted to ensure accuracy of scores and to align rater scoring.

When developed by experienced assessors, assessment centres can be carried out face-to-face, virtually and online, with the development of AI tools also impacting on assessment centre delivery and scoring.

Development Centres

Often people get confused with assessment and development centres. Both generally use the same techniques to evaluate a candidate's or employee's performance, but the difference is the purpose. A development centre, as the name suggests, focuses on the individual's professional development. It assesses strengths and developmental needs with the aim of offering a full report at the end of the programme that includes a well-defined developmental plan for each candidate.

Although utilising the same techniques as assessment centres, development centres are thought to be perceived by employees as a less threatening and an objective way to assess their developmental areas.

Summary

Summary of chapter 7

1. Assessment centres consist of a combination of different exercises (some psychometric and some non-psychometric)

2. Assessment and development centres are similar – with development centres being for development purposes and therefore some activities or assessment methods may be less appropriate.

3. Consult with subject matter experts if in doubt as to how to build an assessment and/or development centre.

Chapter 8

The predictive power of assessments

THIS CHAPTER COVERS:

- The use of different assessment methods, traditional and non-traditional, as well as the predictive validity associated with the different methods.

The figure on the next page provides an indication of the most effective assessment methods in predicting outcome variables such as performance and job success, using data from a variety of different studies. It is evident that the most popular methods are not necessarily the most predictive. If organisations are still using less reliable predictive methods it may be due to a variety of factors such as cost implications, time availability, a lack of resources, and less buy-in from business on the effectiveness and necessity of reliable, valid and predictive assessments. It is then no surprise to hear that some companies are still struggling to successfully recruit the right people, with the right capabilities for the right roles.

Predictive Validity	Popularity
1.0 (Highly predictive)	100% (Highly popular)

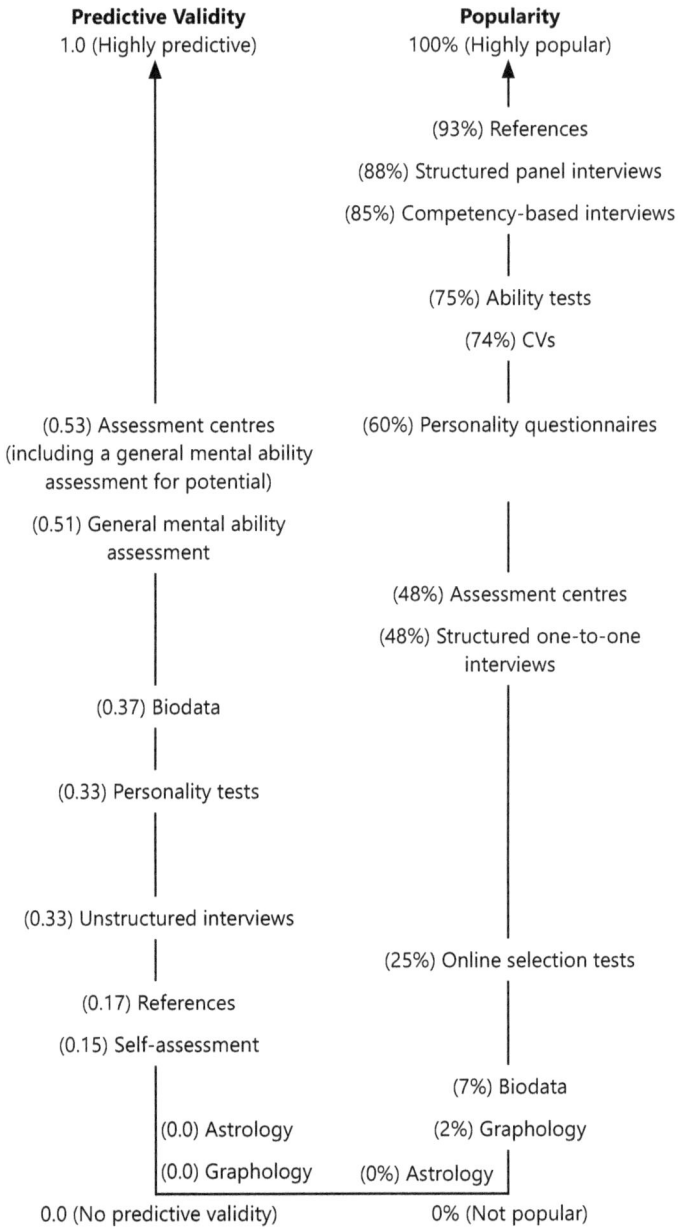

Figure 7: Predictive Validity versus Popularity of Common Assessment Methods

Compiled using data from Beruta, Anderson & Salgado, 2005; CIPD, 2000, 2006; Gaugler, Rosenthal, Thornton & Bentson, 1987; Hunter, & Hunter, 1982; McDaniel, Whetzel, Schmidt & Hunter, 1998; Reilly & Chao, 1982; Robertson & Kinder, 1993; Schmidt & Hunter, 1998; Shackleton & Newell; 1991.

The popularity of some assessments is surprising despite their lack of predictive validity. We know that predictive validity refers to the degree to which an assessment can accurately predict outcomes related to an outcome variable such as performance, and although some assessment methods have been utilised for many years, studies have provided empirical evidence to suggest that they are not as accurately predictive as people believe them to be.

In the late 1970s, it is reported that the United States had over 3000 companies using graphologists (handwriting analysts) as personnel consultants, whilst in Europe 85% of hiring decisions were made using graphology despite research illustrating that it has little to no predictive validity.

From figure 7, it appears that some of the most popular assessment methods appear to be the least predictive of job-related outcomes while some of the most predictive methods are less popular. For example, if we look at reference checks, many companies rely on references to make a hiring decision. However, research has shown that these have very poor predictive validity. Conversely, if we look at assessment centres, which are the most predictive means of assessing candidates, when included with a mental aptitude assessment, they are much less popular – around the 50% mark.

The more predictive the methods, the more likely you are to attract and retain the individuals who contribute meaningfully to organisational performance. As you compile an assessment battery using different assessments, especially those that show higher levels of predictive validity, you increase the predictive validity compared with utilising just one assessment alone.

When weighing up the costs against the benefits of using predictive assessments, the calibre of candidate that makes it through to the final interviewing stages is likely to be a lot higher. If it requires more resources, increased financial investment or more time spent on carefully deciding on the organisation's selection process, the benefits are bound to outweigh the costs – especially when considering the cost of poor hiring decisions as discussed in Chapter 2.

Summary of chapter 8

1. The most popular assessment methods are not always the most reliable.

2. Using assessment centres that include a general mental ability test have the highest predictive validity.

3. Some assessment methods should not be utilised for selection and development purposes.

Chapter 9

Optimising the candidate experience

....

> **THIS CHAPTER COVERS:**
>
> ■ Key factors to consider to improve the candidate experience of your selection process.

When conducting talent assessments, what employers fail to consider is the impression that is left with candidates after their interactions with the organisation; be it through an interview, assessment or assessment centre. Some employers leave candidates with memories of a really bad experience, while other candidates leave with nothing but good things to say about their interactions following the selection process. In addition, potential candidates could become potential clients later down the line and research has shown that most job applicants are more likely to buy from a company that provided a good candidate experience when they applied to work there. In conducting the selection process there are many factors to consider, some of which you may have already considered, while others may help you optimise your current selection process.

Factors to consider in conducting the selection process

....

1. Make the process applicant-friendly

The candidate experience begins with the application process, and this is the stage at which you can instantly build (or lose) trust in potential employees, as we are said to live in a world where candidates choose companies just as much as companies choose them. The application process should not be complicated, repetitive or time-consuming, as employers begin to shift towards more simplified global application systems. Ensure that the process is engaging, intuitive for candidates, and available on multiple platforms as jobseekers will have access to browse for jobs using their smartphones.

2. Pre-screen to filter potential candidates

Screening candidates can be very time- and resource-intensive, especially when you receive hundreds of applications for every role advertised. By pre-screening candidates based on minimum requirements such as qualifications, experience, and skills, you may end up rejecting over half of the applications even before the interview stage. This allows you to sort the applicants who are more suited to the role over those who are less suitable in a quick, cost-effective manner. One of the cautions with using pre-screening solutions is to ensure that you are not ruling out candidates on criteria that are advantageous, but not essential, as you could miss out on or decline talented candidates.

Pre-screening solutions can take on many different forms, from pre-screening questionnaires that candidates complete before submitting their application, to telephonic pre-screenings, pre-screening assessments or even background checks. Ensure that the selection process you choose to follow is in line with the legislation of the country in which you are utilising the pre-screening tools.

3. Positively position your brand

The company needs to have an application portal and career site which is easy to navigate and allows people to learn more about the company, mission, roles available and employee value proposition. Website content is particularly important because it is said to be the signpost or image of the business, giving candidates a sense of what the company is about. Some employers have dedicated web pages for potential employees who wish to join the company even if roles are not available, leaving candidates feeling like their skills are valued and important without necessarily being tied back to a particular position. When running assessment centres employers forget that they are showcasing the organisation, not just when they are introducing themselves to candidates but also through the way they engage with other assessors and the way in which they engage with candidates during and after the assessment centre.

When candidates experience a professional and well-run assessment centre, even if they felt under pressure to perform, they walk away feeling challenged, and those who enjoy challenge look forward to working for your company.

4. Connect with high potential applicants

Whether you have decided to hire the candidate or not, it's essential to connect and keep in touch with candidates who performed well and displayed potential through the selection process. This creates a positive impression on candidates as it can come across as a genuine interest in their development, which it should be. If they accept another role, you never know when they may apply to your organisation again, thereby creating a "passive" candidate pool of talent.

5. Provide personalised feedback

Instead of a standard rejection letter or email, take the time to mention what you liked about them and where they can focus their development – especially related to the role. Let them know you'd like to get back in touch with them when a suitable position is available in the future and ask them if they would be open to that. Providing feedback to candidates can be really beneficial, especially for those who are new to the job market, as candidates are generally open to the development feedback. By providing feedback in declining a candidate it is always good to take note of behaviours and reactions following a regret-letter as individuals may feel less inclined to act in a favourable manner. Surprisingly, you may receive some extremely mature responses, and in some instances, you may receive an email which reflects a candidate in a very different light to the way they displayed themselves during the selection process. In the same light, be sensitive and professional in the way you position the feedback to promote development.

6. Ask candidates for feedback

It may come as a pleasant surprise when employers ask candidates for feedback on how they experienced the selection process, an assessment centre or an interview. It not only gives you insight into ways to enhance the process, from individuals who do not have a vested interest in the organisation, but also allows you to reflect on improvements that could be made.

A structured hiring process that provides an applicant-friendly experience and cultivates a positive impression of your employer brand builds trust in potential employees. This is key to drawing the right candidates to your organisation.

Summary of chapter 9

1. Candidates are also marketers of your business, as they share with others their experience of applying and interacting with your organisation.

2. Connect with candidates who display high performance and potential during the selection process as they may look to join your organisation later – if not as an employee then possibly as a client. Some may even refer other good candidates to your company.

3. Provide feedback to candidates and gain their feedback on how the selection process can be optimised.

Endnotes

1   Cappelli, P. (2008). *Talent Management for the Twenty-First Century.* Retrieved from: https://hbr.org/2008/03/talent-management-for-the-twenty-first-century

2   Adamsen, B. (2016). The Etymology of the Term 'Talent'. In *Demystifying Talent Management* (pp. 77-87). Palgrave Macmillan, London.

3   Silzer, R., & Dowell, B. E. (2010). Strategic talent management matters. *Strategy-driven talent management: A leadership imperative*, 3-72.

4   Ernest R Hilgard, Ernest R (1965). "Robert M. Yerkes Biography". *National Academy of Sciences* : 1-43.

5   Uhlaner, J. E. (1977). *The Research Psychologist in the Army – 1917 to 1977* (No. ARI-RR-1155-REV). Army research institute for the behavioral and social sciences, Alexandria, Virginia.

6   Ernest R Hilgard, Ernest R (1965). "Robert M. Yerkes Biography". *National Academy of Sciences*: 1-43

7   Benjamin Jr, L. T., & Baker, D. B. (2014). *From séance to science: A history of the profession of psychology in America.* University of Akron Press.

8   Brigham, C. C. (1922). *A study of American intelligence.* Princeton: Princeton University Press; London: Oxford University Press, c1922 to 1923.

9   Gould, S. J. (2014). *A nation of morons.* Retrieved from: http://www.garysturt.free-online.co.uk/gould.htm

10 American Educational Research Association, American Psychological Association, National Council on Measurement in Education, Joint Committee on Standards for Educational, & Psychological Testing (US). (1999). *Standards for educational and psychological testing.* American Educational Research Association.

11 Sabel, J. (2017). *Is your assessment 50 years old? A brief history of assessments.* Retrieved from: https://www.hirevue.com/blog/is-your-modern-assessment-50-years-history

12 Zielinski, D. (2018). *Predictive Assessments give Companies Insight into Candidates' Potential.* Retrieved from: https://www.shrm.org/resourcesandtools/hr-topics/talent-acquisition/pages/predictive-assessments-insight-candidates-potential.aspx

13   Sabel, J. (2017). *Is your assessment 50 years old? A brief history of assessments*. Retrieved from: https://www.hirevue.com/blog/is-your-modern-assessment-50-years-history

14   Ash, P. (1966). The implications of the Civil Rights Act of 1964 for psychological assessment in industry. *American Psychologist, 21*(8), 797.

15   Sabel, J. (2017). *Is your assessment 50 years old? A brief history of assessments*. Retrieved from: https://www.hirevue.com/blog/is-your-modern-assessment-50-years-history

16   Zielinski, D. (2018). *Predictive Assessments give Companies Insight into Candidates' Potential*. Retrieved from: https://www.shrm.org/resourcesandtools/hr-topics/talent-acquisition/pages/predictive-assessments-insight-candidates-potential.aspx

17   Almog, G. (2018). *Traditional Recruiting Isn't Enough: How AI is Changing the Rules in the Human Capital Market*. Retrieved from: https://www.forbes.com/sites/groupthink/2018/02/09/traditional-recruiting-isnt-enough-how-ai-is-changing-the-rules-in-the-human-capital-market/#4354b5f8274a

18   World Economic Forum. (2016). *The 10 skills you need to thrive in the Fourth Industrial Revolution*. Retrieved from: https://www.weforum.org/agenda/2016/01/the-10-skills-you-need-to-thrive-in-the-fourth-industrial-revolution/

19   Mercer. (2019) *Global Talent Trends 2019*. Retrieved from: http://www.mmc.com/content/dam/mmc-web/insights/publications/2019/feb/gl-2019-global-talent-trends-study.pdf

20   Mercer. (2018) *Global Talent Trends 2018 Study*: Unlocking Growth in the Human Age. Retrieved from: https://www.mercer.com/content/dam/mercer/attachments/global/webcasts/gl-2018-pdf-global-talent-trends-study-us-canada.pdf

21   Mercer. (2019) *Global Talent Trends 2019*. Retrieved from: http://www.mmc.com/content/dam/mmc-web/insights/publications/2019/feb/gl-2019-global-talent-trends-study.pdf

22   Mercer. (2018) *Global Talent Trends 2018 Study*: Unlocking Growth in the Human Age. Retrieved from: https://www.mercer.com/content/dam/mercer/attachments/global/webcasts/gl-2018-pdf-global-talent-trends-study-us-canada.pdf

23   Mercer. (2019) *Global Talent Trends 2019*. Retrieved from: http://www.mmc.com/content/dam/mmc-web/insights/publications/2019/feb/gl-2019-global-talent-trends-study.pdf

24 Mercer. (2018). *Global performance managemnent survey*. Retrieved from: https://www.mercer.com/products/performance.aspx

25 Sherbin, L., & Rashid, R. (2017). Diversity doesn't stick without inclusion. *Harvard Business Review, 1*.

26 Schwartz, J., Collins, L. & Stockton, H. (2017). *The future of work: The augmented workforce: 2017 Global Human Capital Trends*. Retrieved from: https://www2.deloitte.com/insights/us/en/focus/human-capital-trends/2017/future-workforce-changing-nature-of-work.html

27 Schwartz, J., Collins, L. & Stockton, H. (2017). *The future of work: The augmented workforce: 2017 Global Human Capital Trends*. Retrieved from: https://www2.deloitte.com/insights/us/en/focus/human-capital-trends/2017/future-workforce-changing-nature-of-work.html

28 Michaels, E., Handfield-Jones, H. & Axelrod, B. (2001). *War for Talent*. Retrieved from: https://hbswk.hbs.edu/archive/war-for-talen

29 Hunter and Hunter (1984) describe the first application of VGA to selection data, and present the first 'league table' of selection and promotion methods.

30 Hunter and Hunter (1984) describe the first application of VGA to selection data, and present the first 'league table' of selection and promotion methods.

31 Mercer. (n.d.). *The value of assessments in Talent Selection and Development*. Retrieved from: https://www.mercer.com/content/dam/mercer/attachments/global/Talent/Mercer_Value_of_Assessments.pdf

32 Mercer. (n.d.). *The value of assessments in Talent Selection and Development*. Retrieved from: https://www.mercer.com/content/dam/mercer/attachments/global/Talent/Mercer_Value_of_Assessments.pdf

33 Accounts + Legal. (2019). *Average employee costs SMEs £12,000 to replace*. Retrieved from: https://www.accountsandlegal.co.uk/small-business-advice/average-employee-costs-smes-12-000-to-replace)

34 Network Recruitment (2015). *The Cost of a Bad Hire*. Retrieved from: https://www.networkrecruitment.co.za/blog/the-cost-of-a-bad-hire

35 HR Review. (2014*). It costs over £30K to replace a staff member*. Retrieved from: www.hrreview.co.uk/hr-news/recruitment/it-costs-over-30k-to-replace-a-staff-member/50677

36 HR Review. (2014*). It costs over £30K to replace a staff member*. Retrieved from: www.hrreview.co.uk/hr-news/recruitment/it-costs-over-30k-to-replace-a-staff-member/50677

37 Frith, B. (2016). *Confidence in psychometric assessments rises*. Retrieved from: https://www.hrmagazine.co.uk/article-details/confidence-in-psychometric-assessments-rises

38 Frith, B. (2016). *Confidence in psychometric assessments rises*. Retrieved from: https://www.hrmagazine.co.uk/article-details/confidence-in-psychometric-assessments-rises

39 Frith, B. (2016). *Confidence in psychometric assessments rises*. Retrieved from: https://www.hrmagazine.co.uk/article-details/confidence-in-psychometric-assessments-rises

40 Frith, B. (2016). *Confidence in psychometric assessments rises*. Retrieved from: https://www.hrmagazine.co.uk/article-details/confidence-in-psychometric-assessments-rises

41 Bragin, N. (2018). *Fortune 500 top hiring trends in 2019. How big corporations hire top talents?* Retrieved from: https://blog.soshace.com/en/2018/09/24/fortune-500-top-hiring-trends-2019-big-corporations-hire-top-talents/

42 Huffcutt, A. I., Conway, J. M., Roth, P. L., & Stone, N. J. (2001). Identification and meta-analytic assessment of psychological constructs measured in employment interviews. *Journal of Applied Psychology, 86*(5), 897.

Index

A

ability tests, 74
alpha test, 4–5
analyses, 13, 17–18, 33, 64
  factor, 48
  running, 52
  statistical, 46, 48
APA (American Psychological
    Association), 4, 7, 32

applicant-friendly, 77, 80
aptitude assessments, 19, 29
  mental, 75
aptitude tests, 44
  common, 44
artificial intelligence, 11, 16, 23,
    40–41
assessment and development
    centres, 69, 71–72
assessment centre delivery, 71
assessment centres, 8, 28, 37, 65,
    69–72, 74–76, 78
assessment development process,
    46
assessment methods, 24, 37, 65, 67,
    70, 72, 75–76
  effective, 73
  popular, 75–76
assessment practices, 6
  objective, 30
assessment processes, 33, 53
assessment providers, 9, 33, 36
  credible, 46
assessment purposes, 38
assessment space, 40
assessment specialists, 56
assessment techniques, 33, 35, 37,
    41

assessments, 1–2, 4–9, 20–21,
    23–24, 26–46, 49, 51, 53–54,
    56–59, 61, 65–67, 69–70, 73,
    75, 77–78
assessments around the globe, 31

B

Baby Boom generation, 13
behavioural indicators, 65
behavioural Interviews, 63
behavioural observation, 34
Bell-shaped Curve, 56
Beta test, 4, 6
business analytics, 13
business psychologist, 33

C

candidate experience, 9, 77
change management, 17
capitalising on talent analytics, 12
assessment methods, 74
conducting the selection process,
    77
cognitive abilities test, 7
Common assessment methods, 74
competencies, 18–19, 70
  job-related, 2
competency framework, 18–21, 32
competency matrixes, 34
competency-based interviews, 34,
    74
costs of bad hiring choices, 23, 26
construction situation, 8
counterproductive workplace
    behaviours, 46
critical role identification, 30
customising employee

www.ingramcontent.com/pod-product-compliance
Lightning Source LLC
Chambersburg PA
CBHW071112210326
41519CB00020B/6270